CONTENTS

RadioTimes

Editor/writer Mark Braxton
Art editor Nick Wells
Executive editor Alexia Skinitis

Picture editor Roger Dixon
Managing editor
Claire Hollingsworth
RT staff photographer
Don Smith

Head of heritage Ralph Montagu
Repro Rhapsody
Production director
Sharon Thompson
Production manager Steve Calver
Sub-editors Jonathan Bond,
Jonathan Bowman, Gill Crawford,
Sophie Heath, Ron Hewit, Jane Hill,
Patrick Mulkern, Ellie Porter,
Hannah Shaddock

**Managing director,
Radio Times Group** Kathy Day
Editorial director Mark Frith
Publishers Claire Hollingsworth
and Ben Head

Printed in the UK by
Ancient House Press

Images supplied by Alamy, Allstar,
BBC Archive, Getty, Mirrorpix, Radio
Times Archive, Ronald Grant Archive

Photography by Allan Ballard,
Reinhold Binder, Hugo Dixon, Tony
Evans, Mark Harrison, Alan Howard,
Roger Jones, Dmitri Kasterine,
Keith McMillan, Colin Maher, David
Montgomery, Brian Moody, Gary
Moyes, Michael Putland, Chris
Richardson, Christopher Ridley

With thanks to Holly Gilliam and
Python (Monty) Pictures Limited,
Don Smith, Paul Vanezis

Trademarks used under licence
from Python (Monty) Pictures
Limited. Any additional content
provided by Python (Monty)
Pictures Limited, Terry Gilliam
and The Terry Gilliam Archive

Published by Immediate Media
Company London Ltd, Vineyard
House, 44 Brook Green, London
W6 7BT. Published in the United
Kingdom 2019. Radio Times is part
of Immediate Media Company
London Ltd

D1514515

MICHAEL PALIN

66 The very idea of not just talking about Python, but **leaping up on stage dressed as a cardinal shouting 'Nobody expects the Spanish Inquisition'** ... I didn't think that was something people did in their 70s 99

ERIC IDLE

66 It went to something like 93 countries – you can't get your mind round something like that. **The good news is that everybody is silly in the world: they understand daftness.** And I suppose the most amazing thing is it went to America, and it changed American comedy. They just went nuts for it 99

JOHN CLEESE

66 I've just been in Canada doing a tour. I did 14 shows in a month to 28,000 people and **the love and affection for Python is quite extraordinary**, with 60-year-old men with a tear in their eye, literally, saying, 'Thank you for making me laugh all those years' 99

TERRY GILLIAM

66 Our big thing was to get rid of the punchline, and that made a difference because then the sketch was about what was going on within it. **I kind of marvel at how good we were.** And how we had the freedom to get away with murder 99

4

GRAHAM CHAPMAN
66 All we are trying to do is to be funny. As far as the BBC is concerned I think we have been rather successful. They have given us a tin shed in the car park for a production office 99

TERRY JONES
66 It was so stuffy in the 60s. **The class system had a stranglehold…** There are no taboo areas with humour – nothing you can't make fun of. The only criterion is: is it funny? If people laugh, it is 99

MONTY'S MOB
From left: Michael Palin, Eric Idle, John Cleese, Terry Gilliam, Graham Chapman and Terry Jones, in Hitting on the Head Lessons, a 1972 sketch from *Monty Python's Flying Circus*

t is July 1969, and an army of engineers is perfecting preparations for the historic first manned landing on the Moon by crew members of the Apollo 11 mission. The same month, Prince Charles is invested as Prince of Wales, the first American troops are withdrawn from Vietnam and, rather appropriately, *Something in the Air* by Thunderclap Newman is at the top of the UK pop charts.

In and around London, the first film inserts are being shot for a new BBC series planned for later in the year: a slapstick silent film involving Queen Victoria and Prime Minister William Gladstone, and men in superhero costumes walking down an ordinary suburban street... In fact, after the actors involved watch Apollo 11 blast off on TV, they spend the afternoon sweltering in 80°F heat while dressed in mouse costumes...

Fifty years ago, comedy was largely safe and predictable. Sitcoms and sketch shows tended to follow established guidelines and ensured that nothing frightened the horses. That is, until six young men came pogoing along on a huge Renaissance foot and trampled over all those rules and conventions until they were nothing but rubble.

Over five years and 45 episodes, an initially mystified general public would gradually get used to, then come to love, the sight of City gents with wayward walks, deceased parrots, Vikings breaking into song about Spam and dark, grumbling cartoon creatures scuttling through Dalí-esque landscapes. *Monty Python's Flying Circus*, in other words.

But we're getting ahead of ourselves. These were clearly exciting, fervid times, the kind that can generate a cauldron of creativity. But how did the collision of elements that was Cleese, Palin, Chapman, Jones, Idle and Gilliam come to pass?

"How the Pythons got together" is not a short story; more of a heavy tome with copious annotations on every page. But it

is fascinating to see the routes taken by these writer/performers, and how the various shows they landed up in, post-university, all came to be regarded as pioneering works of television, and helped them learn their comedy craft.

Minnesota-born Terry Gilliam was a law unto himself, just as he was very much his own boss on Python. A graduate of Occidental College, Los Angeles, he tried out animations on *Do Not Adjust Your Set*, the much-admired ITV children's comedy that ran from 1967 to 69 and featured the Bonzo Dog Doo-Dah Band (with future honorary Python Neil Innes).

After Oxford, Michael Palin and Terry Jones cut their teeth on *The Frost Report* and *Do Not Adjust Your Set*. John Cleese and Graham Chapman came up through *That Was the Week That Was*, *The Frost Report* and *At Last the 1948 Show*, while fellow Cambridge graduate Eric Idle also did stints on *The Frost Report* and *Do Not Adjust Your Set*.

s a Venn diagram, the pre-Python intersections resemble an incompetent conjuror's magic rings. But what actually brought them together?

Palin recalls, "I remember a quite significant phone call with John Cleese. Terry Jones and myself had just done a series called *The Complete and Utter History of Britain* [Jan–Feb 1969, ITV], of which a few fragments survive. Some of it was very funny and some of it didn't quite work, and John said, 'Well, you won't be doing any more of those, will you?' in his cheerful, supportive way.

"But on the other hand, he was interested in us as performers and writers. We – Terry Jones, myself and Eric – had worked on *Do Not Adjust Your Set*, and John

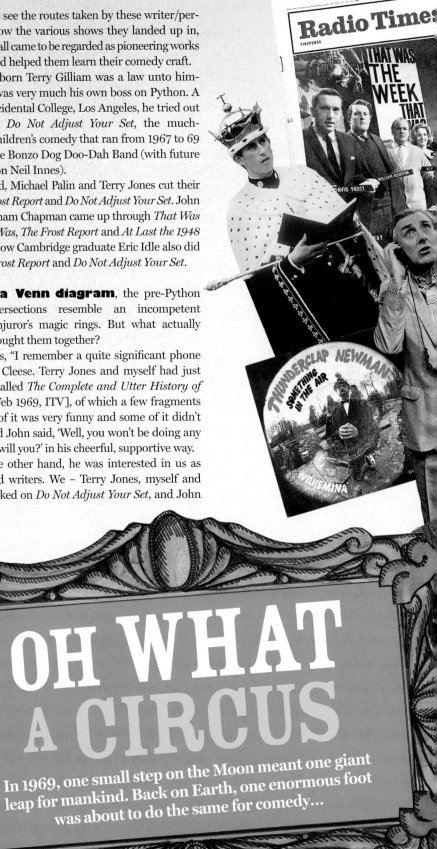

OH WHAT A CIRCUS

In 1969, one small step on the Moon meant one giant leap for mankind. Back on Earth, one enormous foot was about to do the same for comedy...

Radio Times July 10, 1969
Midlands and E. Anglia   July 12-18

Radio Times

EIGHTPENCE
BBC **tv**

TARGET
MOON

Follow this week's histo...

⁶**We started laughing at what we each had written. That was a marvellous moment**⁹

JOHN CLEESE

was the funniest man around at the time – he'd done *At Last the 1948 Show*. We looked at John and Graham Chapman and all those performers and thought, 'These are really good people, we'd love to work with them.' So when John said, 'Is there anything we can do together that would be different and unusual – let's have a talk about it,' that was exciting.

"Of course, it didn't necessarily mean anything *would* work: there were six people chosen fairly randomly, because we all made each other laugh, but it did work and from the first meetings on, there was physically a good mix of people."

The BBC's comedy adviser Barry Took then arranged for the group to meet head of comedy Michael Mills. As Took later told *Radio Times*, "At the time, I felt that television comedy was getting a bit flat-footed and I just had a hunch that by getting them together and giving them their heads, they would have an effect on each other."

What a hunch that was. Given this golden opportunity, however, the new team found that they were severely underprepared. Asked by Mills what they had in mind for a comedy series, they were unable to give definitive answers about guests, music, or very much at all... By Cleese's recollection, it was "humiliating".

However, at the point where the hopefuls expected the meeting to grind to a halt, Mills told them to go away and make 13 programmes. If they were incredulous then, the Pythons remain so to this day. As Palin once told *Radio Times*, "There were no conditions. Nobody said, 'Can we see a script?' Now it has to go through half a dozen stages. They want to know what you're writing about, how long it will take, how much it will cost. It has to be checked for political correctness, 'compliance', 'diversity'. It's much more controlled."

Cleese takes up the story today: "It was nerve-racking at the start because after we'd had this extraordinary meeting with Michael Mills, and without us having any idea, we were anxious for a bit because we had one or two meetings that got absolutely nowhere – until dear old Terry Jones said, 'Well, let's just go home and write.' And then after a few days we had a read-through at Terry's flat in Camberwell [south London], and we started laughing at what the others had written, what we each had written. And that was a marvellous moment."

It was Spike Milligan who indirectly gave the gang the breakthrough they needed. His freewheeling, anarchic comedy series *Q5*, which aired in spring 1969, showed them that they didn't have to be governed by the twin tyrannies of punchline and structure. In other words, it encouraged them to do exactly what they wanted.

Palin and Jones even sought out Ian MacNaughton, who had directed and produced *Q5* and went on to do the same for *Flying Circus* with the exception of 👉

the first four episodes. Those were produced by John Howard Davies, who brought in Carol Cleveland.

Thereafter, everything else fell into place, if somewhat slowly. The programme title had a famously problematic birth, for example. Among the names they toyed with were *It's*, followed by *It's Not*; also *Arthur Megapode's Cheap Show*, *Vaseline Parade* and *The Venus De Milo Panic Show*. Other notables included *Whither Canada?*, *Owl Stretching Time*, *A Horse, a Spoon and a Bucket* and *You Can't Call a Show Cornflakes* (Idle's favourite).

The BBC started referring to the proposed show as *Barry Took's Flying Circus*, the last part of which the group liked, and this was added to a made-up name for a sleazy theatrical agent, with one of the group suggesting "Python" and another, "Monty".

Gilliam came up with the surreal opening titles, a world of fast-growing flowers, unicycling clergy and inflating heads, plus of course the famous "Foot of Cupid" – a cutout taken from Agnolo Bronzino's 1545 painting *Venus, Cupid, Folly and Time*.

The first studio recording of *Monty Python's Flying Circus* took place on Saturday 30 August, in Studio 6 at BBC Television Centre, after a warm-up by Barry Took. This would end up being episode two. "The day of recording I've always remembered very, very clearly," says Cleese today, "because the first sketch was the one about the flying sheep, and I remember waiting in the wings to watch Terry and Graham do it. I was with Michael and I said to him quietly, 'We could be the first people in history to record a comedy show to complete silence.' And he said, 'I was having the same thought.' We had no idea how it was going to be received. And people always say, 'Did you think it was going to be a great success?' Absolutely not!"

Anxiety was clearly a predominant emotion among the Pythons that day. As Gilliam told *Radio Times* on the show's tenth anniversary, "My only memory is just the audience arriving there and people thinking that they'd come to see a circus... We arrived, and there was this queue of people outside waiting to come in – all keen. And the BBC was calling it a circus, so I think it was just a family audience and old age pensioners coming to see the lions and the clowns."

For Palin, the emotion was more akin to terror: "It was a feeling, not exactly of jumping off a cliff on a dark night, but certainly of being slowly pushed off. You really didn't know quite what you were getting into..."

Chapman was more confident, it seems, after all the work that had already gone into the show: "I didn't really care about the studio audience, provided people were looking happy at the end – I liked the material so much."

And as it transpired, Cleese and Palin, still in the wings at this point, started to relax: "There were one or two chuckles," says Cleese, "and then a laugh. And then a

WHEN THE MEMOS FLEW

23 December 1970, the day after series two ended with a particularly problematic episode, and Aubrey Singer, head of the BBC Features Group, objected to the Undertakers sketch written by John Cleese and Graham Chapman

big laugh. And I remember thinking, 'It's going to be all right.'"

The circus was up and running, though it would be some time before it was really flying (see Paul Fox, right). Making its debut on BBC1 on 5 October 1969, the first series was initially given a graveyard slot on Sunday nights, never before 9.45pm and even relegated to 11.25pm one week.

Today, Palin says, "We very much felt we were on the margins of the BBC's output and the BBC encouraged us to feel that way. They didn't put a great deal of money into it, they scheduled the show quite late at night for fear of children seeing it, I think, and if ever anything else of the BBC's standards overran, Python would be the one that suffered. So we were put to one side, shown late, taken off, we were a regional opt-out in certain parts of the country... But looking back now, I think it all helped enormously. It allowed us to create 13 shows, six and a half hours of television, virtually unscrutinised by the BBC. And although we didn't have huge audiences, we did by the end have quite a loyal cult following."

Idle agrees, "It was a small, late-night show, nobody knew what it was, so it sort of grew in its own mad space. It found a little area to develop without being noticed."

Cleese adds, "The moment we began to take off was when Alan Coren wrote a glowing review in *The Times*, but not until they repeated the first series. It started to get a real following – not a very big following compared with Morecambe and Wise, but it was enough, that was the point. The man who was in charge of light entertainment, a man called Tom Sloan, thought it was absolutely awful – as he told dear old Ian MacNaughton in the lift! But there were enough people who liked it. And then it began to gain a little bit of impetus. And then it began to take over our lives..."

Watching the show today on Netflix or DVD, it's hard to appreciate how alien the sight of dead parrots and Hell's Grannies, to say nothing of Gilliam's cut-and-paste grotesques, must have seemed to British viewers. But before long, this late-night secret was a world-conquering behemoth, on telly, on stage and in the cinema.

1969 was a very busy year, then. But while a padded boot on the Moon is as far as manned space exploration has ever gone, Cupid's foot made sure that comedy, and TV in general, would never be the same again.

John Howard Davies

4050 T.C.

"MONTY PYTHON'S FLYING CIRCUS"   2846/7   14th October 1969

Ian McNaughton

If you should by any chance use the Marriage Guidance Counsellor again as a VT insert please let me know because David Frost's address has been mentioned in it and would have to be changed. We have already used his phone number and Tom Sloan and the Postmaster General have already had my balls, and in fact if I give you a caption I would be very grateful if you could record it with a Cleese voice over after the show so that I may cut it into episode one in order to avoid being castrated a second time when the programme is repeated.

Copy to: Ian Macnaughton

27th November 1969

Dear John,

Firstly let me congratulate you on the success of the series. The shows seem to me to be getting better and better and this is a view that is shared by most people who see it.

This letter is to confirm the arrangements that I would like to propose to you for next year, which I believe were discussed verbally with Barry Took before he left for beautiful down-town Burbank. We shall finish making the first 13 on 4th January, 1970, and transmit the last of the 13 on 11th January, 1970. We intend to repeat these on BBC 1 on Fridays from week 17 (1st May to 24th July). We would like to begin recording the second series in week 14 - namely 5th April (with filming beginning at an approximate number of weeks before that). We would then like to record these next 13 on the following dates:-

Sunday, 5th April, 1970.   Sunday, 12th April, 1970.
Saturday, 18th April, 1970.   Sunday, 26th April, 1970.

...and mysteri...

10.55 *New series*
Monty Python's Flying Circus
Whither Canada
Conceived, written and performed by
Graham Chapman, John Cleese Terry Gilliam, Eric Idle Terry Jones, Michael Palin
Make-up supervisor JOAN BARRETT
Costume supervisor HAZEL PETHIG
Animations by TERRY GILLIAM
Designer ROGER LIMINTON
Produced by
JOHN HOWARD DAVIES †
and IAN MCNAUGHTON
Will Mr Monty Python collect £200?: page 6

11.25
Weatherman

Closedown

...PETER BUTTERWORTH
...STERKE
ll..........HAROLD BERENS
.........THELMA RUBY
by JACK TREVOR STORY
he novel *All On The*
r by JACK LINDSAY
JAY LEWIS
J JACK HANBURY

Memo from the top...

Paul Fox, controller of BBC1 1967–73, separates myth from the reality of Python's birth

The first time *Monty Python's Flying Circus* appeared in the programme pages of *Radio Times* was on Sunday 5 October 1969. There it was at 10.55pm, just after *Omnibus* and before the weatherman. "New series," it said, "conceived, written and performed by Graham Chapman, John Cleese, Terry Gilliam, Eric Idle, Terry Jones, Michael Palin." The *Radio Times* proof on my desk kills at least two canards about the series: it began on BBC1, not on BBC2; it began as a network programme and not as a regional opt-out.

The mythology about how it arrived on BBC1 screens has grown over the years. The facts are that Barry Took, then a consultant to BBC comedy, got the project together. It was his idea to team John Cleese, then in *The Frost Report*, and Graham Chapman, with Michael Palin and Terry Jones. Palin and Jones had been appearing on ITV in *Do Not Adjust Your Set*, an early-evening programme, and they were then joined by Eric Idle, followed by the American cartoonist Terry Gilliam.

It was the late Michael Mills, then head of BBC comedy, who brought it to me with some trepidation. "It's a bit anarchic, it's a bit silly, it can be quite funny, it is certainly different," was the summary of his recommendation to me to give it a six-week run.

With the new autumn season already under way, the only available time for *Monty Python* was late on Sunday night. There wasn't much argument at that time about its slotting: everyone knew we were attempting something new. The era of satire was over: they set out to make us laugh – in a completely different way.

At first, there were divided views on whether they succeeded. Within the BBC there were senior executives who felt that the programmes were going over the edge of what was acceptable. Others made it clear that the series was at times dazzling and full of some very good things. As for the public, some were puzzled; some were cautious; some saw it as enormously funny; and some thought it was just stupid.

The second series, 12 months later, went out in London only at 10.10pm on Tuesday nights. The rest of the country saw it on other nights. The Monty Python team were disappointed by this split transmission pattern. But their upset was slight compared to the outrage felt by the viewing public. Clearly, I had made a mistake to schedule it in this half-baked way and by the time the third series came along, all was well. Monty *Python's Flying Circus* was networked at a good time on a good night – and the rest, as they say, is history.

This article appeared in the 18 November 1989 edition of Radio Times

THE FULL MONTY...

TERRY GILLIAM

Born 22 November 1940
Minneapolis, Minnesota, USA

Python roles The staff animator, responsible for titles, links and extended cartoons. Also frequently called upon to play faceless drones such as a medieval knight who would bring sketches to an end by braining characters with a rubber chicken. Overeating layabout Kevin Garibaldi (the "Beans! Beans!" man) is another monstrous highlight.

Silliest moment "We were on Dartmoor filming a superhero sketch called Mr Neutron, and I had to rush into this tent, as an American dialogue coach, and show Graham how to say, 'OK'. And I couldn't remember what an American accent was. I was terrible."

Other career highlights After co-directing Monty Python and the Holy Grail with Jones, he went on to direct solo projects including Jabberwocky, Time Bandits, Brazil, The Adventures of Baron Munchausen, The Fisher King, Twelve Monkeys, Fear and Loathing in Las Vegas and recently The Man Who Killed Don Quixote.

Cleese on Gilliam "Terry would go off and do his wonderful work and we wouldn't see it until the day of the recording. He didn't play parts requiring dialogue because he could only do very strange voices."

GRAHAM CHAPMAN

Born 8 January 1941, Leicester
Died 4 October 1989, Maidstone

Python roles First and foremost, the Colonel, a British Army officer who interrupted proceedings when they became "too silly", which was often. He played many other authority figures, and cut an imposing Mr Neutron. Considered by the others to be a very fine actor, he went on to front their films The Holy Grail and Life of Brian.

Silliest moment "My favourite memory is the Undertaker sketch. John and I laughed more while we were writing that than anything we ever did, I think. The BBC got a bit jumpy after that one."

Other career highlights A qualified doctor, Chapman wrote with Cleese for the Doctor sitcoms on ITV, and also wrote for comedian Marty Feldman, with whom he collaborated on pirate film Yellowbeard.

Jones on Chapman "Douglas Adams [the author and scriptwriter] said that Graham was extremely... in fact he was one of the most extremely people he knew. And I think he's right. He didn't do anything by halves. Graham was a surprising man. In the same way that he surprised us into laughter, he surprised us into love for him."

JOHN CLEESE
Born 27 October 1939
Uphill, Weston-super-Mare, Somerset

Python roles The announcer, always in formal attire, who sits at a desk (wherever that may be) and gets to say the immortal line "And now for something completely different"; the aloof, meticulous Eric Praline, who rigorously investigates malpractice, in sketches including Crunchy Frog and Dead Parrot; and of course the Minister of Silly Walks.

Happiest moment "My happiest moment was the first time I read out Cheese Shop to the others."

Other career highlights Co-writing and starring in *Fawlty Towers*, writing and starring in *A Fish Called Wanda*, taking the lead in *Clockwise*, playing Q's assistant R, then Q himself, in two James Bond films and Nearly Headless Nick in two Harry Potter films.

Palin on Cleese "One of the great joys of the 2014 Python reunion [at the O2 Arena] was John. Just seeing him in dreadful drag, enormous bosoms, awful skirts, legs apart talking about penguins on the TV. He was collapsing with laughter. It was joyous."

TERRY JONES
Born 1 February 1942
Colwyn Bay, Conwy

Python roles The Naked Organist, the archetypal "Pepperpot" (a term invented by Chapman for the screeching, middle-aged women that all of them played), the increasingly repetitive Spam waitress, and East End gangster Dino Vercotti, brother of Luigi.

Silliest moment "One of the silliest moments was when we were making *Life of Brian* and I was the hermit who sat in the hole, and my costume consisted of a long beard and nothing else."

Other career highlights Co-writing *Ripping Yarns* with Palin, directing three Python movies (one with Gilliam), then *Erik the Viking*, *The Wind in the Willows* and *Personal Services*. A historian, Jones has written books and hosted documentaries on the Crusades, Rome, Egypt, medieval lives and the Barbarians.

Palin on Jones "As soon as I met him I realised that Terry was very funny and friendly and generally easy to get on with."

11

ERIC IDLE

Born 29 March 1943
South Shields, Tyne and Wear

Python roles The double-entendre-obsessed man in "Nudge Nudge", Mr Badger, a Scotsman who interrupts sketches without warning, and holiday-seeker Mr Smokestoomuch. The musically gifted Idle wrote many of the group's famous songs, too.

Silliest moment "The Fish-Slapping Dance, when Michael falls about 20 feet into the water. It perfectly represents the relationship between John and Michael."

Other career highlights Creating *Rutland Weekend Television* and the spin-off film *The Rutles*, starring in *Nuns on the Run*, *Splitting Heirs* and *Casper*. He wrote the lyrics and book for the stage musical *Spamalot*, and created and directed the 2014 sell-out Python reunion shows at the O2.

Palin on Idle "Eric has always been a very gregarious character, as long as I've known him. He was always very popular, with loads of friends around him."

MICHAEL PALIN

Born 5 May 1943, Sheffield

Python roles The tattered and torn "It's Man", impetuous Cardinal Ximénez ("Nobody expects the Spanish Inquisition!"), the cross-dressing Lumberjack, downtrodden husband Arthur Pewty, the shades-and-pinstripe-wearing Luigi Vercotti, and assorted prevaricating shopkeepers.

Silliest moment "When I had to leap into an E-Type Jaguar and drive it along some very narrow Scottish lanes dressed as the front half of a pantomime horse. It was thoroughly dangerous and one of the most stupid things I've ever done."

Other career highlights Co-writing *Ripping Yarns* with Jones, writing and starring in *The Missionary*, co-writing and starring in *American Friends*, starring in *A Private Function* and TV's *GBH*, fronting travel documentaries including *Around the World in 80 Days* and *Pole to Pole*, and latterly profiles in art history.

Idle on Palin "Michael is very, very nice. A very, very nice man. Too nice sometimes. He hates upsetting people."

CAROL CLEVELAND

Born 13 January 1942
East Sheen, south London

Python roles Philandering wife Deirdre Pewty, the bride in Buying a Bed, a nurse in Me Doctor, Mrs Attila the Hun, Joseph Montgolfier's fiancée Antoinette and various "Glamour Stooge" roles (her term). She was in most *Flying Circus* episodes and all Python films.

Funniest moment "I loved the Hell's Grannies. A favourite sketch I was in was the Semaphore Version of *Wuthering Heights*."

Other career highlights Appeared on TV in *The Saint*, *The Avengers* and *Randall and Hopkirk: Deceased*, worked with comedians Mike Yarwood, Lenny Henry and Kelly Monteith, starred in films including *Vampira* and *Funny Money* and appeared in numerous stage productions.

Palin on Cleveland "I don't think Carol gets enough credit. She was just so good at what she did, and she was just so unerringly right for whatever she did. We were very lucky to have someone who pinpointed the humour so well. She had a great sense of fun."

NEIL INNES

Born 9 December 1944, Danbury, Essex

Python roles Joined *Flying Circus* for the final series to write sketches and songs, was an important part of the stage shows and composed music for *The Holy Grail*, appearing as Brave Sir Robin's cheeky minstrel and a page who was squashed by the catapulted Trojan Rabbit.

Funniest moment "The day the script for *Holy Grail* came through the letter box. I lay down on the sofa to read it. When I got to the Black Knight duel, I suddenly realised I was rolling around the floor and slapping it with laughter. No other script has had this effect."

Other career highlights Part of the Bonzo Dog Doo-Dah Band, who had a hit with *I'm the Urban Spaceman* and appeared on *Do Not Adjust Your Set*, where they met Idle, Jones and Palin. Featured in and composed the songs for *Rutland Weekend Television* and *The Rutles*. Had his own show, *The Innes Book of Records*.

Palin on Innes "He's an essentially social member of the Python team on the road. Neil's songs are the only things that go down unequivocally well wherever we play. He's very versatile... No. I'll tell you the truth. He has a shameless love of dressing up, that's what he loves!"

13

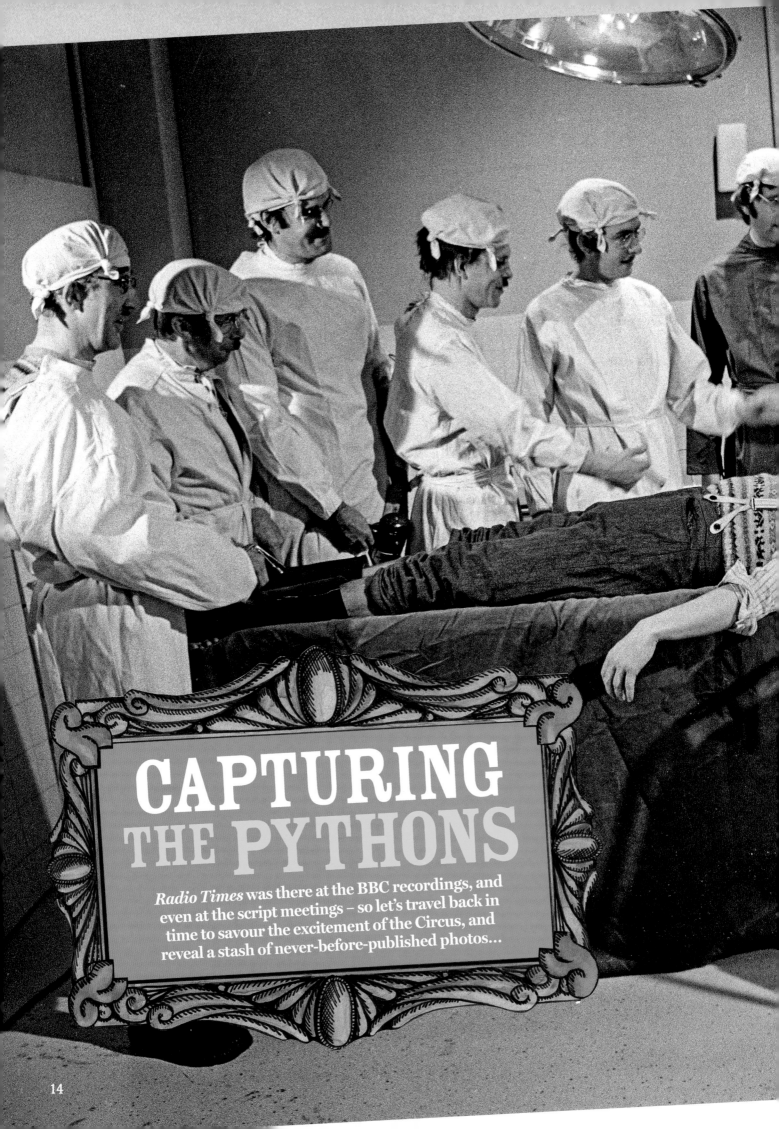

CAPTURING
THE PYTHONS

Radio Times was there at the BBC recordings, and even at the script meetings – so let's travel back in time to savour the excitement of the Circus, and reveal a stash of never-before-published photos…

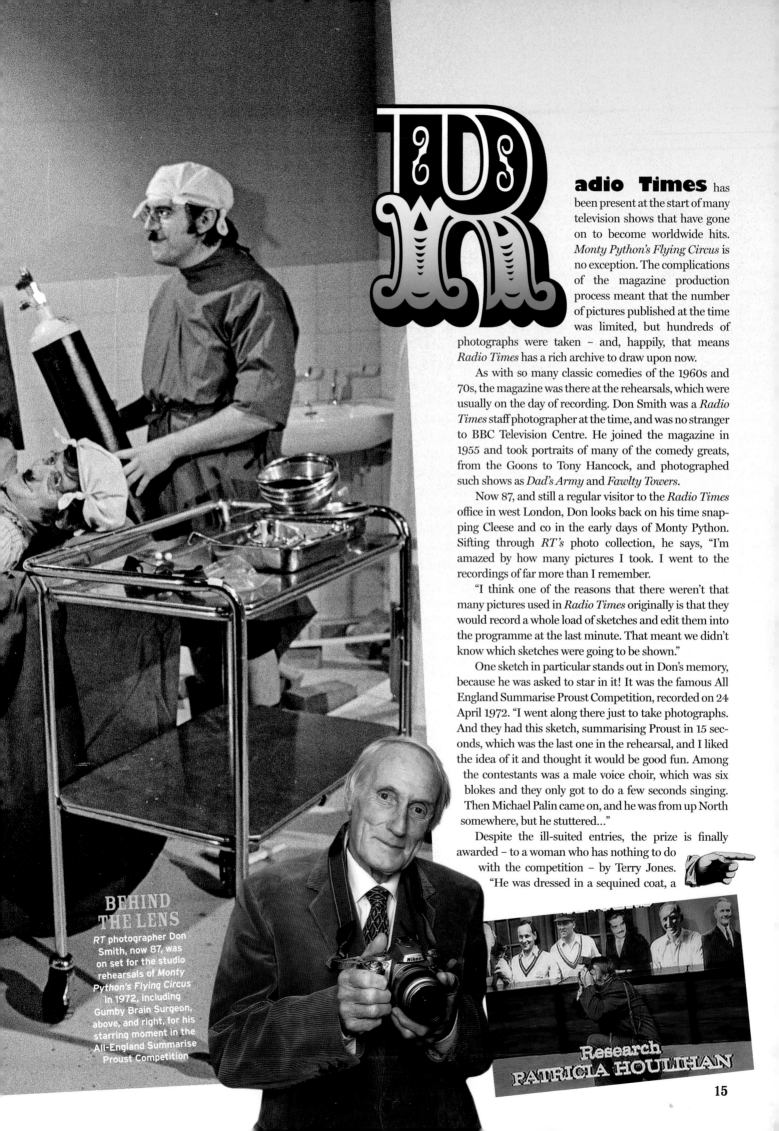

Radio Times

Radio Times has been present at the start of many television shows that have gone on to become worldwide hits. *Monty Python's Flying Circus* is no exception. The complications of the magazine production process meant that the number of pictures published at the time was limited, but hundreds of photographs were taken – and, happily, that means *Radio Times* has a rich archive to draw upon now.

As with so many classic comedies of the 1960s and 70s, the magazine was there at the rehearsals, which were usually on the day of recording. Don Smith was a *Radio Times* staff photographer at the time, and was no stranger to BBC Television Centre. He joined the magazine in 1955 and took portraits of many of the comedy greats, from the Goons to Tony Hancock, and photographed such shows as *Dad's Army* and *Fawlty Towers*.

Now 87, and still a regular visitor to the *Radio Times* office in west London, Don looks back on his time snapping Cleese and co in the early days of Monty Python. Sifting through *RT's* photo collection, he says, "I'm amazed by how many pictures I took. I went to the recordings of far more than I remember.

"I think one of the reasons that there weren't that many pictures used in *Radio Times* originally is that they would record a whole load of sketches and edit them into the programme at the last minute. That meant we didn't know which sketches were going to be shown."

One sketch in particular stands out in Don's memory, because he was asked to star in it! It was the famous All England Summarise Proust Competition, recorded on 24 April 1972. "I went along there just to take photographs. And they had this sketch, summarising Proust in 15 seconds, which was the last one in the rehearsal, and I liked the idea of it and thought it would be good fun. Among the contestants was a male voice choir, which was six blokes and they only got to do a few seconds singing. Then Michael Palin came on, and he was from up North somewhere, but he stuttered..."

Despite the ill-suited entries, the prize is finally awarded – to a woman who has nothing to do with the competition – by Terry Jones. "He was dressed in a sequined coat, a

BEHIND THE LENS

RT photographer Don Smith, now 87, was on set for the studio rehearsals of *Monty Python's Flying Circus* in 1972, including Gumby Brain Surgeon, above, and right, for his starring moment in the All-England Summarise Proust Competition

Research
PATRICIA HOULIHAN

15

very glitzy thing, doing the typical host bit," Don continues. "That was the end of the sketch and it was the end of the show as well. This was in the afternoon. Then almost immediately there was some discussion, and someone suggested when the prize is announced they ought to have a photographer rush on and take pictures. Of course, I was standing there and somebody said to me, 'Would you be prepared to do it?' And I was quite flattered, quite pleased. It also meant I had to stay on for the evening recording. Which I did.

"I told the floor manager and also the cameramen that I was going to go into their final shots, because they wouldn't have expected me to do it. I was always behind them. That was agreed. So, in the evening performance, we got to awarding the first prize, then I dashed on – but it was only in the last four or five seconds of the sketch!"

The green-jacketed Don is seen scooting on to snap the winner, in front of the judges, who are cut-outs of five cricketers, plus actor Omar Sharif and violinist Yehudi Menuhin. It wasn't the last time Don effectively played himself in a TV comedy; he also got the call during an episode of the 1990s sitcom *Absolutely Fabulous*.

So we've had a glimpse into the recordings, but *RT* was also invited to those fertile periods of comic creativity, the planning sessions and script meetings. The first time we did so was during the second series in 1970, watching the Pythons at play in a club hall in East Acton, not far from BBC TV Centre, although only portrait shots of the cast exist from that day.

Producer/director Ian MacNaughton would sit at one end of a trestle table covered with scripts, which the Pythons would then leaf through, sometimes bursting into fits of giggles. "As long as we are still laughing at rehearsals, then it stays" was the rule that MacNaughton operated by.

The group tended to work in pairs – Cleese with Chapman, and Palin with Jones – apart from Idle and Gilliam, who were lone operators. "Everyone came from a different angle on it," says Palin today. "John and Graham were slightly more aggressive, in a sense, Terry and I were the two sillier ones, Eric was brilliant on the verbal sketches, the music and all that. So everyone had something to contribute.

6 As long as we are still laughing at rehearsals, then it stays 9
IAN MACNAUGHTON, PRODUCER

"And I think one of the most important aspects of Python at that time was getting Terry Gilliam involved, because as an animator he was quite brilliant and we'd worked with him before on *Do Not Adjust Your Set*. He managed to bring to this group of disparate British comics a certain sort of American style, sharp and classy, that enabled us to put remains of sketches together. He would be, if you like, the putty between the sketches. He was able to supply the links that enabled us to make a show that was not conventional in any way. Everybody caught everybody else's sense of humour; no one was playing catch-up at the time."

Towards the end of the Pythons' time on *Flying Circus*, photographer Christopher Ridley was asked by *Radio Times* to take candid shots of their preparations for the fourth and final series in 1974, featuring musician Neil Innes but minus Cleese. Ridley, now aged 79, who is the father of *Star Wars* actor Daisy Ridley, doesn't remember any specific sketches that they were working on, "more a mêlée of creative fragments". And although there were no dominant personalities, he describes the newly introduced Innes as "a very talented musician – the Rutles, Doo-Dah Band – he collaborated musically and creatively, so he's putting in his ha'penny worth there."

Innes remembers being brought into the Python fold like this: "Eric rang and asked me to come up to the TV Centre – their warm-up man was ill. I said, 'I don't do warm-ups!' He said, 'It pays 25 quid.' I said, 'Done!'"

Ridley is a big fan of the Python brand of humour, and of this period in comic and cultural history. "I was working as an

assistant to Lewis Morley, and was an assistant on the Christine Keeler photo, the famous nude one with the chair," he says. "Morley's studio was on the top floor of the Establishment club with Peter Cook and lovely Dud. A wonderful zeitgeist and it was great to swim in it like a fish with a bit of privileged access, and add my bit, hopefully. It was a great time to be in London."

But it wasn't just at work that the photographers met the Pythons, as Don Smith remembers. A musician in his spare time, Don and his jazz band were once hired to play at a Victorian house in Highgate in north London... "The first person I met there was John Cleese. He probably thought, 'Why are you here? Are you going to take photographs?' But I had a double bass with me, and it was obvious I wasn't. He didn't know I played. It turned out that the house was Graham Chapman's."

Of all the Pythons, the two that Don encountered most of all – mainly for their subsequent

SAY CLEESE
John Cleese gets the giggles in a 1972 rehearsal of the Off Licence sketch, and below, in 1974, Neil Innes (right) takes instruction from Ian MacNaughton (left). "Top beret modelling," says Innes

meetings were very good fun and it was always a bit tricky because people would have to play politics about whether to read out the first sketch after lunch when everybody's fast asleep after a pint or two, so that was always a sticky period and sometimes things would go badly because of the way that they were read!"

Inevitably, among six very different people, there were tensions, often between Jones and Cleese. And things going wrong were a source of worry – even in the first sketch ever recorded involving a moustache that wouldn't stick. But as Palin explains, "I realised as we went on that when things went wrong the audience absolutely loved it, so that was our safety net." There were even mistakes in the 2014 O_2 Arena gigs, including, once again, a droopy moustache, "but there were absolute roars of laughter," adds Palin.

Not every sketch made the grade, of course, but the meetings were usually fruitful, and the breakthroughs were memorable, as John Cleese now tells *RT*. "The happiest moment I had in Python was when Gray [Graham Chapman] and I had spent a lot of time writing the Cheese Shop sketch and I kept losing confidence in it and Gray kept on just saying it's funny, it's funny. When I finally read it out, it didn't really take off to begin with. Then suddenly Michael started to laugh and he got quite out of control, and actually fell off his chair. And he was lying there on the floor howling with laughter."

> **6 Michael started to laugh, and he actually fell off his chair 9**
> JOHN CLEESE

The incident is also Idle's funniest memory: "I just remember that moment very strongly, of Michael going completely, and losing it. And John, when he loses it completely, would lie on the floor and bang his feet on the floor... this enormous chap lying on the floor just completely howling with laughter. And that's what happened with the writing, that's why the writing sessions were more fun. It's the first time we heard most of those sketches entirely, so the audition was to see if we could make ourselves laugh. If it made us laugh, we'd put it in the show, and if it didn't we sold it to *The Two Ronnies*."

Seeing pictures of those 1970s script meetings, the relaxed smiles and postures, one can only speculate at just how much fun the Pythons had together, bouncing gags and ideas off each other. As Eric Idle succinctly put it, "We were a bit like a great football team. Very different individuals, but stick us on the football field and we were fantastic."

SERIES

1

1969-70

FIRST IMPRESSIONS

TV critic Philip Purser previewed the first episode of
Flying Circus in *Radio Times* in October 1969, describing
it as coming from "the school of hairy comedy"

RADIO TIMES 2 OCTOBER 1969

This Sunday, the very latest in a long line of late-night shows on BBC1 passes 'Go.' After watching all the moves, we didn't dare make any comment ourselves but instead asked TV critic Philip Purser for his. His views are, of course, his own!

Will Monty Python collect £200?

Monty Python's Flying Circus: Sunday 10.55 BBC1

The object of the game . . . but let's not pretend 'Monotony' is for playing. It's just a way of reminding you of the rise and fall of the late night show, and of some of the people who played it for real kicks, real ha'pence and real telephone calls. Leaving aside a premature ITV attempt called *What the Public Wants* (either the public didn't or if it did, didn't get it for long), the saga began with *That Was The Week That Was*, abbreviated to TW3.

Perhaps because it was the first, it now seems easily the best. It was all so revolutionary—newsy lyrics to the songs that Millicent Martin sang, sketches hammered out on the typewriter that day, pomposity and hypocrisy mocked. David Frost crouched at the centre of operations, with his insolent hair style and delivery that was a sort of running parody of popular communication.

Bernard Levin was severe to all sorts of people, one of whom eventually took a swing at him (and missed) while another, a lady astrologer, squirted him with a plastic lemon.

After a second season with TW3, the next idea was a more relaxed session three nights a week, with the jokes and lampoons padded out with Lots of Good Talk. This was the era of Harvey Orkin, Norman St John Stevas, John St Harvey Orcas and Orkin St Steven Enormas. It was called *Not So Much a Programme, More a Way of Life*. Next came BBC-3 and a new compere, Robert Robinson, who addressed everyone by their surnames, which was just as well as most of them were called John – Bird, Fortune, Wells, *et al.* Al was also known as Eleanor Bron.

The Johns lingered on into the fifth and really the final manifestation of Saturday night satire, *The Late Show*. Ned Sherrin, who'd produced all the others, then departed for Wardour Street.

A small flame of satire flared up intermittently in the late night reviews which came and went in 1967 and 68, most successfully in *The Eleventh Hour*. Bernard Braden brought along his own brand. But the emphasis was on the school of hairy comedy of John Cleese and Bill Oddie and Graeme Garden, represented first by *Twice a Fortnight* and now again by *Monty Python's Flying Circus*. Last summer, though there was one last nostalgic reunion of some old TW3 talents in *Quiz of the Week*. Even Ned Sherrin was back, as a chairman of great charm and wit. Asked why a busy film producer should bother with such a television show he answered with what is perhaps the neatest justification of the whole satire epoch. He said, 'Well, it keeps me off the streets on Saturday night.'

Game devised by WILLIAM RUSHTON
Illustrations by NIGEL HOLMES

22 And, having said that, here are your players. Cut them out, mount them on a ha'penny (told you the game was unplayable!) and proceed to Old Kent TW3. Bottom right, you may seem to see a joker. Not at all. He's soccer commentator Kenneth Wolstenholme, 'compere' of

EPISODE
Whither Canada?

FIRST TRANSMISSION

Sunday 5 October 1969
10.55pm BBC1

A new era in TV comedy, and television in general, begins in suitably improbable fashion, with Michael Palin's bedraggled castaway taking a full 51 seconds to emerge from the sea, stagger up to the camera and croak, "It's!" Starting as it means to go on, the programme offers up a potently surreal concoction with such ingredients as Wolfgang Amadeus Mozart (right) presenting **Famous Deaths** (including Lord Nelson falling from a tower block), classical composer **Arthur "Two Sheds" Jackson** finding it impossible to discuss his work seriously (bottom), and **The Funniest Joke in the World** being explored for its military potential (below).

ON THE EARLY DAYS, PALIN SAYS,

66 There's an opening sketch where I thought, 'This is the beginning of the end for Python'. It was only the first show we recorded! It's where John and I have to share a moustache when we're playing the two people talking about the Anglo-French Concorde Sheep. When you finished speaking you had to take the moustache and stick it on the other person, who would then start speaking. And the moustache kept falling off. It was completely hopeless. **We giggled, we had to do retakes, nobody knew what was going on** 99

EPISODE
Sex and Violence

FIRST TRANSMISSION
Sunday 12 October 1969
11.05pm BBC1

An early, hit-heavy instalment features **Flying Sheep** (right), Arthur Frampton, the **Man with Three Buttocks**, Eric Idle's inappropriate **Marriage Guidance Counsellor** getting sidetracked by Carol Cleveland on her debut, The World around Us investigating the growing epidemic of men wanting to be mice, and the existence of God being determined by a bout of wrestling between a monsignor and a humanist. Gilliam is on knockout form, with his homicidal perambulator and the sculpture of **Rodin's Kiss** turning out to be a Dutch organ.

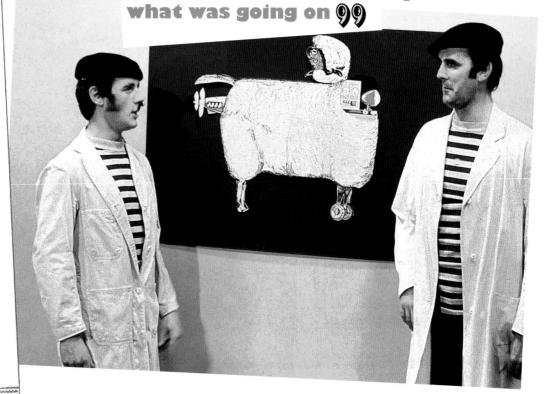

HERE TO ETERNITY

On 25 November 1969, Palin and Cleese rehearse the sketch about a deceased Norwegian Blue parrot that will gain everlasting life in the comedy pantheon

OF THE DEAD PARROT SKETCH, PALIN SAYS, 66 Python for some reason or other is lodged in the national subconscious, and will be there for a long while, I suppose. **And we're doomed to have the Parrot sketch played back at us for the rest of our lives.** But it's not a bad thing to be remembered for... 99

EPISODE 8

Full Frontal Nudity

Episode title not billed in RT

FIRST TRANSMISSION
Sunday 7 December 1969
10.45pm BBC1

A private asks Chapman's Colonel for permission to leave the Army after just one day – before he gets killed – gangsters Dino and Luigi impose their **Protection Racket** on the same Colonel (opposite, far right), and newlyweds who are **Buying a Bed** (above, right and opposite, bottom left) are thwarted by a salesman who multiplies every figure by ten and another with an aversion to the word "mattress". The legendary **Dead Parrot** sketch (pages 28-29) airs for the first time, and takes a diversion via a British Rail complaints office (opposite, centre). An already immortal episode ends with **Hell's Grannies**, which Carol Cleveland loved: "The idea of old ladies going around beating up young people was rather appealing."

EPISODE 9

The Ant, an Introduction

Episode title not billed in RT

FIRST TRANSMISSION
Sunday 14 December 1969
10.55pm BBC1

A semi-musical lecture on **Llamas** is topped by a man who can play *La Marseillaise* by sticking a finger up his nose, and Cleese brilliantly performs another of his "eccentric behind a desk" turns – this one, a man who sees two of everything, is interviewing for a **Mountaineering Expedition**. Palin's blood-stained barber proves his inherent unsuitability for the role in a story that builds into the **Lumberjack Song** (the "best girl" by his side is played by Cleese's wife, Connie Booth, above with Palin). And Idle is on fine form with his obsequious compere Kenny Lust, and as an unwelcome guest in **The Visitors**.

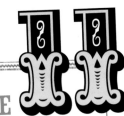

EPISODE 10

Untitled

FIRST TRANSMISSION
Sunday 21 December 1969
11.10pm BBC1

A dramatic, intensely acted "It's" from Palin, hung like a pig carcass in an abattoir, kicks off this action-packed episode. A plumber receives a letter from the BBC inviting him to appear in a sketch. **Arthur Tree** (an actual tree) presents his own show, ushering in a forest of wood-based puns. (The Larch is back, by the way.) And Ron Obvious (right) fails to become **The First Man to Jump the English Channel**. At **Pet Conversions** (above), a customer wanting a cat is presented with a terrier, and there's an interview for a **Gorilla Librarian**. The promised programme Yes, It's the Sewage Farm Attendants, never materialises. Thankfully. A series of unlikely animal interactions from Gilliam, presented as a bizarre way to end the show, reflects a certain self-awareness from the team.

Christmas Night with the Stars

FIRST TRANSMISSION
Thursday 25 December 1969
6.45pm BBC1

The Pythons were asked to chip in to this annual festive extravaganza, although their contribution ended up being a repeat of **Confuse-a-Cat** from episode five. The sketches originally intended for this slot ended up in other episodes anyway, including as they did Pet Conversions (episode ten), a Charles Atlas animation (five) and the unwelcome visitors (nine). Legend has it that the original line-up was not felt to be in the festive spirit. The segment as aired was introduced by Val Doonican as "This is Monty Python's Circus…" Also on the bill were *Dad's Army*, Dick Emery and Mary Hopkin.

EPISODE 11

Untitled

FIRST TRANSMISSION
Sunday 28 December 1969
11.25pm BBC1

A string of letters of objection, each complaining about its predecessor, follows some lavatorial humour, before a detective inspector continually corrects his own grammar in an **Agatha Christie** drawing-room scene. In **Interesting People**, a Bicycle Choir performs *Men of Harlech*. Undertaker gags and scantily clad women then predominate, until the **Batley Townswomen's Guild Presents the Battle of Pearl Harbor** (left), essentially an excuse for the cast to put on dresses and thrash about in a muddy field. It's a favourite of Terry Jones, who told *RT*, "It was such a liberating sketch to perform."
Series one continues on page 34

Letters

Why no 'Monty Python' in the Regions? Why end 'Quiz of the Week'?

Why are we in the North to get *The Great North Road Show* on BBC1 on Tuesday evenings instead of *Monty Python's Flying Circus*? Why can't the South get the music-hall and pipes that we've got sick of hearing?

Monty Python is the best comedy you've ever shown, even if it is repeats, and I'm not the only one who thinks so. Why not show *The Great North Road Show* later on for everybody, and save us the frustration of knowing what we're missing and not being able to do anything?

B. Aitken
Whitehaven, Cumberland

Another from the North
I must complain about not being able to get the best comedy programme on the television, *Monty Python's Flying Circus*, on Tuesdays at 10.

While the rest of the country is watching *Monty Python*, we are getting some queer programme about Geordies. I must tell you Teesside is *not* in Geordie land, and does not want to be, so can we please get *Monty Python's Flying Circus*.

John Davis
Middlesbrough

. . . East Anglia, too . . .
Looking through my RADIO TIMES (London and South-East edition) I decided that the highlight of my limited viewing week would be the return of *Monty Python* at 10 on Tuesdays. But when I switched on to BBC (East Anglia) I was surprised, and rather disappointed, to find my favourite comedy show replaced by *Farming Club*. The nearest I could get to the *Flying Circus* was a frustratingly vague, silent shadow flickering on the London channel.

I am not suggesting that farmers should be deprived of their half-hour of topical interest, but surely in an evening's programmes consisting almost entirely of repeats and American films, 30 minutes of British comedy could have been transmitted nationally?

Is there any hope that East Anglian *Monty* fans will some day have the opportunity of seeing a repeat, or have the parochial pundits in Norwich

decided it is too clever for us?

J. A. White
Sudbury, Suffolk

. . . the Midlands . . .
I greeted with joy the return of *Monty Python's Flying Circus*, but I now find that the Midlands is to receive *Contact*, a boring programme, while others get *Monty*. Why should this be? Do you think we in the Midlands are born without the ability to laugh?

We do not all sit in pubs drinking Brew IX. You must regard us as loyal but ignorant labourers who do not know what we want. Equal rights for the Midlands! We need a good laugh up here.

Trevor Sproston
Birmingham

. . . and the South
After looking forward for some time to the repeat of *Monty Python's Flying Circus* I now find that we in the south will not be able to receive it. Instead, we are treated to yet another documentary programme on local affairs. The BBC tried hard to discourage *MPFC* addicts from watching the initial series by putting it on at about 3 am. Are we to be ignored again? I believe a new series is starting in the autumn. Will we be able to see it?

I suppose we will be forced to watch *Farm Progress* or the News in Welsh. If so, I had better move to the Orkneys or the Outer Hebrides to see the best and most original comedy series ever.

Michael Paul
Weymouth

PAT BEECH, Controller English Regions, replies: *The BBC planned to introduce a weekly local programme from each of its Regions on Tuesdays at 10 pm. Three have started this year; five follow next year.*

Regional topical material is already shown at 6 pm; the extra outlet needs to be later in the evening to allow for different types

of programmes. To get any sort of regional showing it must replace something in the schedules. Controller BBC1 keeps these under continuous survey, but whatever he drops someone is bound to be disappointed.

'Quiz': outside the 'norm'
The moment a programme begins to show invention outside the 'norm' the BBC seems to drop it. The latest victim, *Quiz of the Week*, was often boring, sometimes childish, very irreverent, but for all that it was t...

Anne Chisholm takes a trip with Monty Python's Flying Circus

The super zany comedy show

Monty Python's Flying Circus: Tuesday 10.0 BBC1 Colour

If you saw **Monty Python's Flying Circus** when it was first shown late at night last winter, the chances are you're hooked already. If you didn't, you are going to have a chance to catch up. For *Monty Python* is making the big time. A new series of 13 programmes starts on BBC1 in August and, as an hors d'oeuvre, five of the original programmes are to be shown again.

Funny television programmes aren't easy to describe on paper: they need to be watched. *Monty Python* is topical, but not party political, and episodic without being a revue. The programme's mood is surrealist, full of fantasy, without being escapist or whimsical. All of which sounds very pompous and would distress the cast of *Monty Python* very much.

Apart from John Cleese (the tall one) none of the cast (who are also the writers) is exactly a household face – yet. In fact although they have to put up with famous John, the others (or at least one of them) feels that it is better for them to be interchangeable, so that it is the show that has the comic personality rather than individuals. But particular roles do emerge, by some sinister unconscious selection process: Terry Jones tends to turn up in slippers with curlers, Graham Chapman seems drawn to play the uptight politician or psychiatrist who freaks out before your eyes in mid-pundity. One of the most endearing aspects of the programme is that it frequently

Terry Gilliam: 'often quite cruel'

sends up other television programmes. The gritty news programme, the meaningful arty interview, the pretentious documentary – *Monty Python* has it in for them all.

And then there's the animation. Terry Gilliam, a small American with the look of a groovier Adam Faith, has made a real success of that. To prove it he carries around a notebook with 'I AM AN AWARD-WINNING ANIMATOR, EVERYBODY!' written on the cover in big red letters. His style of animation uses cut-outs, usually from old prints or engravings; it is simple, he explained, and cheap, which is a help. Rather than having to make lots of little pictures of people in different positions, with cut-out animation you can just move the pieces around. *Monty Python* contains some of the cleverest animation ever to reach a wide adult audience in this country – and it is an integral part of the programme. It is also ravishingly pretty, and often quite cruel. Terry Gilliam says that with cut-out, you just do find yourself cutting off people's heads, legs, hands and so on. It's a simple movement,' he explained, smiling happily.

'It's not easy to be very subtle.' Snip, snip.

The producer, Ian Macnaughton, made a serious effort to explain what they are doing. 'We have tried to choose the five (of the old series) which will lead best into the slightly different style of the new series.' What style? 'The style that came out of what we were doing towards the end.' 'Zany' is his, and the cast's, favourite adjective for their programme. They have tried to pick the zaniest of the first lot to prepare us for the super-zaniness of the next. 'The main thing,' said Terry Jones after an afternoon spent watching run-throughs of the last series, during which everyone laughed uproariously at their own best bits, ' is to get people realising that the show is – a funny show.' It is.

> "*Monty Python* is the best programme you've ever shown," wrote a reader, one of many complaining about regional opt-outs during the repeat run in 1970. Also that year, Terry Gilliam explained his art, with his pet cat, "Cat", on his shoulders...

12

EPISODE

Untitled

FIRST TRANSMISSION
Sunday 4 January 1970
11.15pm BBC1

Two office workers watch a succession of colleagues falling past their window, Professor Tiddles of Leeds University is unable to present his research into "Things", and Mr Hilter and Ron Vibbentrop plan their campaign for the **North Minehead By-Election**. The energetically played **Upper Class Twit of the Year** competition (right), filmed at Hurlingham Park in Fulham, south-west London, ensures more sketch-show immortality, while consumptive courtier **Ken Shabby** reassures Rosamund's father of his honourable intentions (not), and a Party Political Broadcast on Behalf of the Wood Party goes disastrously awry.

13

EPISODE

Untitled

FIRST TRANSMISSION
Sunday 11 January 1970
11.10pm BBC1

A woman who doesn't like this, or that, or indeed anything, enters a **Cannibal Restaurant**, where a semi-naked Jones proudly claims, "I'm the special". Cleese's shouty ice-cream saleswoman tries to get rid of her **Albatross** (left), while Idle's pidgin-English-speaking **Me Doctor** confuses everyone. The Gumbys take part in **Historical Impersonations**, Probe-Around explores the subject of crime, while Attila the Hun gives himself up to police for looting, pillaging and sacking a major city. A leading surgeon, meanwhile, operates on a man who keeps hearing music and finds squatters in his body. "What a terrible way to end a series," a Gilliam animation announces, before being squashed by the trademark *Monty Python* Bronzino foot.

SURTEES 2. 1970

EPISODE 5

FIRST TRANSMISSION
Tuesday 27 October 1970
10.00pm BBC1

Palin's ingratiating game-show host presents an episode of **Blackmail** (right) with a nude Gilliam on the organ (not Jones, as one might expect), the AGM of the **Society for Putting Things on Top of Other Things** ends in disillusionment, and the Pythons interact with one of Gilliam's more anatomical animations. Meanwhile, Idle is an unwitting guest in the **House That Destroys Itself**, and a documentary about **Boxer Ken Clean-Air Systems** offers the kind of throwaway visual gag for which the show is becoming famous. After an interview with Ken's elderly mother in a wheelchair, the camera pans back to reveal that she is sitting on top of a car, which then drives away...

EPIS...

FIRST...
Tuesda...
10.10p...

The A...
featuring...
the US s...
Show, do...
the Secr...
Affairs (...
and Mr...
by the co...
interesti...
who inst...
The New...
of Two C...
parrots)...
and wo...
Idiot...
of Engla...
Finally,...
known...
the hos...
blow o...

SILLY PARTY

5% 4% 3% 2% 1% 0 1% 2%

EPISODE 6

FIRST TRANSMISSION
Tuesday 3 November 1970
10.10pm BBC1

A school prize-giving soon becomes a war zone in LF Dibley's latest film, **If**; a posh dinner party is interrupted by the delivery of three hundredweight of dung; and in **Timmy Wilson's Coffee Time**, Idle's David Frost soundalike sparks huge laughs and applause from the studio audience. The official in a **Registry Office** believes he is being propositioned, and a gruesome Gilliam fairy tale begins with a woman using a tiny decapitated man as lipstick. Bringing up the rear, the classic **Election Night Special** – with Sensible and Silly Parties vying for power (left) – exercises the team's knack for inventing ridiculous names.

Before he became enveloped in the madness of *Monty Python's Flying Circus*, John Cleese nearly embarked on a solicitor's career. Here Irma Kurtz describes the goings-on at a *Monty Python* planning session . . .

'Let's have a silly picture,' suggested tiny, grey John Cleese

Monty Python's Flying Circus: Monday 10.10 BBC1 Colour

'RIGHT!' said John Cleese, consulting a piece of paper on which something appeared to be written. 'Here's how it stands: shopping, silly Olympics, history of comedy, restaurant, quickie, fruit . . .'

'Which fruit is that?' Eric Idle asked, looking up from Graham Chapman's shoulder where he was lettering Butch Liberation Front with his pen.

'Killer fruit.'

'Oh. *That* fruit.'

'And ten seconds of,' continued John Cleese, 'sex.'

Cleese rescued

Terry Jones, who has a tendency to burst into unidentifiable songs, burst into an unidentifiable song.

'I find the idea of pursuing a man with a pineapple and then pushing him out of a window and blaming the pineapple very funny,' John Cleese said, which was understandable. It was also understandable to learn that John Cleese was rescued not that long ago from a career as a solicitor in a very posh law firm in the City.

At rare moments, when the sunlight caught his fine profile or when he snarled, he looked like a solicitor, a demented solicitor albeit, who reads the law books for their laugh lines.

There is something legal about his stature, which is very tall most days although some days, he says, he is less tall. Especially when he's trying to be imperturbable and bring order, when he is doing his imitation of a father figure among juvenile delinquents, he resembles the man of law he

trained to be. 'Oh, please Cleese, please! Don't be serious!' said Graham, admonishing.

A visitor to their planning session, where more is undone in five hours than 50 business executives could undo in five weeks, begins in a state of mild confusion, which after a few hours becomes utter.

'We think of ourselves,' John Cleese said, 'as writers-stroke-performers.'

'Let's have a silly picture,' John Cleese had said to me on the phone. 'And let's not talk about how I feel about Vietnam.'

Yet, after we had chatted together at the bottom of Terry's garden where there are, I was assured, a few renegade fairies, John Cleese himself talked about war and about Vietnam, about all sorts of grown-up things, and he talked with feeling and fluency. He even talked about marriage.

His own took place over three years ago to an American actress called Connie. They had two ceremonies, the first before an American Justice of the Peace who rattled the whole thing off so quickly that John and Connie Cleese only realised they had been joined for life when they distinguished the words: '. . . nowmarriedfivedollars.'

Monty Python's Flying Circus is the most uproarious, the silliest thing that has happened to Britain in years, maybe since *Tristram Shandy*, certainly since licensing hours.

To look at the *Monty Python* team, I would never have guessed that they were, in fact, insidious: Terry Jones, bright-eyed and as sweet in appearance as Typhoid Mary must have been; Eric Idle,

looking more like a pop star than an epidemic; Michael Palin with his disarming freckles; Graham Chapman with the deceptive claptrap of a pipe-smoker spread out in front of him on the table waiting to be assembled into a Sherman Tank. And John Cleese.

'Ve haff vays of making you laff!' said Eric Idle as I settled back on the leather sofa trying to make nonsense of what they were saying.

Eric, who longed to go into the sunny garden and play, fidgeted, eyed his guitar which had been put too high for him to reach, sighed. I realised that despite the buffoonery they were actually working quickly and ideas were being shared and each would take his portion home, work on them, polish them, write them and have them in shape for the next meeting.

Lunch was announced by an imaginary gong, because Terry had fetched hot food from a local Chinese restaurant. It is only on such oriental occasions that lunch is announced by an imaginary gong. Normally, I was told, it is announced by the grinding of five sets of teeth on bone.

Chopsticks flash

Chopsticks flashed and the conversation was not slow. The combined academic achievement around the garden table was great, certainly enough to drive most men sane and it is a tribute to the inherent lunacy of our system of higher education that no one in the *Monty Python* team can be called anything like chronically serious, despite their clutter of

doctorates and masters' degrees.

Among the five present – and Terry Gilliam, the dazzling animator and cartoonist who was not at the meeting – each does what he is best at, which means what he likes to do, and outside their *Monty Python* activities they lead separate and independent lives with separate interests, passing as normal, fun-loving citizens among their neighbours.

'Make it silly'

'We're called silly,' John Cleese said with pride. 'Silly is irresponsible, but it's a childish irresponsibility. Silly is an innocent word, like naughty.'

Michael Palin, for personal reasons, began to auction off the last fried prawn.

'I don't want it,' Graham said.

'Nobody wants it,' Eric said.

'What if that happened at Sotheby's with a Degas? What if they brought it out and nobody wanted it?' Mike asked.

'Take away your Degas! Put it back in the box!' cried Eric.

'Bring on the prawn!' John Cleese pounded on the table. 'We want the prawn!'

Michael raised the prawn, bit into it.

'It's a forgery,' he said.

'Make it silly enough,' John Cleese told me, waving an editorial finger, 'and it's news.'

Opposite: PC Graham Chapman hatchets Michael (the clown) Palin. Terry Jones (top) is amused; Eric Idle and Carol Cleveland are concerned only with posing, John Cleese with being tiny and grey

RADIO TIMES DATED 5 AUGUST 1

Greet early
for Christmas.

RADIO TIMES DATED 5 AUGUST 1971

For this 1971 *Radio Times* feature, a picture was taken of the Python cast including John Cleese, but in the end, one with a suitably "silly" cutout of him was chosen.

1972

Monty Python's Fliegender Zirkus

Between series in Britain, the Pythons were invited to Germany by a Bavarian TV producer, Alfred Biolek, with a view to creating a show there. The resultant glossy, 45-minute special boasted new sketches written in English and translated into German. The team had to learn their lines phonetically.

Subjects included a guide to **Albrecht Dürer**, a bovine **Merchant of Venice** and the Silly Olympics – plus a specially adapted **Lumberjack Song**. German critics liked the show – broadcast in Germany on 3 January 1972 – enough that a second was commissioned, but this time it was shot in English and translated into German. Gilliam offered bespoke titles, and the running order included **Chicken Mines of North Dakota**, **The Philosophers' Football Match** and **The Tale of Happy Valley**. It was broadcast on 18 December 1972.

Locations for *Fliegender Zirkus* included the football pitches of the Bayern Munich team and Neuschwanstein Castle, built for Ludwig II of Bavaria – and used in the film *Chitty Chitty Bang Bang*. Recalling the shoot in his diary, Palin wrote: "It's a perfect day for throwing a dummy of John Cleese from the 100ft tower of the castle to the courtyard below."

Monty Python's Fliegender Zirkus was eventually shown in the UK on 6 October 1973, but only the second episode.

TEUTONIC TALES
The Tale of Happy Valley, filmed at Neuschwanstein Castle in southern Bavaria, starred, from left, Idle, Palin, Connie Booth, Chapman, Gilliam, Jones and Cleese

The Pythons enjoyed the beautiful Bavarian surroundings – not to mention the Schnapps (see overleaf) – and flourished in the freedom, creating longer, more filmic sketches. **IN THE PHILOSOPHERS' FOOTBALL MATCH, ERIC IDLE** as Socrates was particularly pleased with his diving header from a cross by Cleese as Archimedes. As he says in *The Pythons Autobiography*, **❝ I keep telling Gary Lineker**, and he keeps promising he's going to show it in the best goals of the last millennium ❞

POSSE PYTHON

Prospectors head for the hills to rake in the rewards of chicken mining. Terry Gilliam (second from left) showed off some impressive horseriding, and enjoyed doing his own stunts, but landed painfully on his gun at one point

Schnapps with everything

It was only when they were 400 schnapps in, as Michael Palin remembers it, that the *Monty Python* team, on their first working trip to Germany, were dropped the news that every word they uttered was going to have to be in German. Everything. Whether it was about bats being hit on the head with teaspoons, or kangaroos' bottoms.

But the schnapps kept on coming and they got through it. That was last year. This year **(Monty Python's Fliegender Zircus Saturday 9.45 pm BBC2)**, it is back to English, with the 'knackwursts' and 'eine kleines' dubbed on later, which Palin says wasn't half as much fun, but easier.

Now, apart from hazy recollections of a hundred stories that he says always sound pathetically lame in the retelling, all he's got to remind him of the German trips are a stein that he can't stand drinking out of, and a yellowing scroll certifying against all the odds that an acquaintance hasn't been to the toilet in five years. In the new one he's a fairytale prince with a false nose that got in the way of his between-scenes tippling.

In Bavaria they came across the perfect castle: Neuschwanstein, all gargoyles and turrets. 'Only trouble was,' Palin says, 'that Visconti had just been there before us and, with his lot's effect on the Gothic fittings, they really weren't too pleased to see us.

'Perfect. Chucking John Cleese off the battlements. The American tourist brigade, standing under the walls with their mouths gaping, thought it was some kind of terribly ethnic folk festival.'

Python's Michael Palin: memories of knackwursts and gargoyles and schnapps

Mike Terry

9.45 *Colour*
Monty Python's Fliegender Zircus
Written, conceived and performed by

John Cleese, Graham Chapman Terry Gilliam, Eric Idle Terry Jones, Michael Palin
Also appearing
CONNIE BOOTH, HERMAN RABBIT

Producer THOMAS WOITKEWITSCH
Director IAN MACNAUGHTON
A Bavaria Atelier GMBH, Munich production for WDR
Schnapps with everything: page 4

QUICK ON THE DRAW

Cleese (above) and Palin (left), drawn by Mike Terry, as they appeared in *RT* for the British debut of *Monty Python's Fliegender Zircus* (or "Zircus" as *RT* spelt it) on 6 October 1973

SERIES

3

1972-3

EPISODE

FIRST TRANSMISSION
Thursday 19 October 1972
10.15pm BBC1

New, plumbing-based titles from Gilliam lead straight into the courtroom, where multiple murderer Michael Norman Randall apologises to the court so eloquently that he's given a six-month suspended sentence. The Icelandic epic serial **Njorl's Saga** is compromised by input from the North Malden Icelandic Society. **Mrs Premise and Mrs Conclusion** meet in the launderette and debate dead-pet disposal and Jean-Paul Sartre. And **Whicker's World** visits a very crowded Whicker Island (above and right), with overlapping presenters droning on about "colonial Campari-land" and "waterfalls of whisky". It's a quintessential sketch, much repeated to represent Python wackiness.

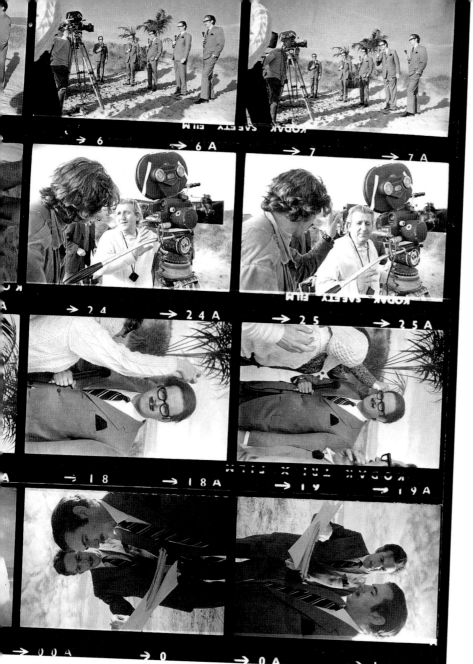

PALIN ON THE FISH SLAPPING DANCE:

"I've seen it so many times, and it never ceases to make me smile. I showed it to my guide in North Korea [the subject of his Channel 5 documentary in 2018]. It's the only time she saw anything of my previous work – she didn't know anything about me at all. **And she just looked at it for a bit, she was a bit puzzled then a big smile broke and she really laughed.** So it's a good ice breaker, that. It's universal "

EPISODE 2

FIRST TRANSMISSION
Thursday 26 October 1972
10.15pm BBC1

After the *Kon-Tiki* and *Ra* expeditions, **Mr and Mrs Brian Norris's Ford Popular** takes them on an epic journey in emigrating from Surbiton to Hounslow; and three *Blue Peter* clones present **How to Do It** ("First, how to rid the world of all known diseases"). Apart from featuring Lulu and Ringo Starr, the episode is also notable for Cleese and Palin performing the **Fish Slapping Dance** (right). The sketch had originally formed part of *Euroshow 71* on May Day of that year.

Page 6

Monty Python's Flying Circus, Thursday 10.15 BBC1 Colour

A new series of *Monty Python* is back this week. Here Michael Wynn Jones talks to artist Terry Gilliam, whose exciting animated cartoons are a major part of the programme's success. 'Where,' asked Wynn Jones, 'do you get the inspiration from?' And with some swift strokes of a felt-tipped pen, Gilliam answered thus . . .

IN Terry Gilliam's studio there is a drawer marked Hands. And another marked Heads. Open them and they spill out on to the floor, hairy clenched fists, fingers groping and pointing and clutching out, heads with poached-egg eyes, with detachable scalps, or with ghastly fixed grins.

The walls are festooned with spare human parts, like a permanent private exhibition of a latter-day body-snatcher: luscious red mouths whose sickly tongues hang limply out for inspection, and feet sawn off at the ankle but still encased in their unmotivated bovver-boots.

Things are not what they seem, of course. The grisly specimens in this mortuary are photographic; enlarged, cut out and restored to a jerky form of life by an ingenious series of hinges and pivots. This is the cast-list, the raw material of Terry Gilliam's macabre cartoons which punctuate the living sketches in **Monty Python's Flying Circus.**

Today they are resting, like their creator who wanders in to see them now and again only to re-vivify them, like Frankenstein, with a cheerful tweak. Not that Terry Gilliam looks like a monster maker. But for the succession of loony incongruities which confront you everywhere in his home, you'd be utterly convinced that behind that disarming, boyish grin nothing but healthy, uncomplicated thoughts were churning over.

But things, as I've observed already, are not what they seem. You take a seat, yet there is something disturbingly uneasy about it. Well, of course, like the one opposite, it's a dentist's chair – and Victorian at that, redolent of who knows what molar agonies?

That flower vase in the corner. Surely it's a gas fire? And the filing-tray, that's a coal-scuttle. That huge piece of machinery on the landing, you'd swear, was the driving gear from an ancient tram, the kind one remembers one's heroes wrestling with in one's youth. Then why is it a light switch? That statuesque lady against the wall can't be – but she is – made out of a gentleman's urinal.

The world outside the window, I assure myself, is going on quite normally. I notice the carrots are coming on beautifully in the window box. Carrots? And onions and radishes. Am I getting disorientated, or did that huge gangling plant in the corner of the box lean over to the vegetable patch, pluck up a young carrot, burp and grow another few inches? Terry Gilliam surveyed the mountains of junk inhabiting his home. 'It was my accountant who advised me to collect junk, said it would be worth a fortune soon. I think I've managed to collect the only junk in the world which in ten years' time will still be junk.'

BUT to business, I thought, so I asked where he got the inspiration for his cartoons. Silence, except for the scratching of a pen . . . . . . Mmm. But what I'd really meant was, what *artistically* speaking was his inspiration? To my vague astonishment he answered verbally.

'Some reviewer said I was descended from Max Ernst. So I bought a book about Ernst and I still didn't understand what he meant. But I did see an exhibition of the surrealist Magritte once. And you know how everyone always gets very sombre in the presence of "art"? Well, I burst out laughing. I hadn't realised what a clown the guy was. He painted some great jokes – like the one about the stone man taking a speck out of another stone man's eye. I appreciated that.'

WHAT are you trying to say in your cartoons, though? Ask a stupid question . . . I pulled myself together and remarked how his cartoons were almost always destructive, bodies exploding quite capriciously or ending in total disintegration.

'That's quite true' he admitted. 'But one's limited by the movement one can create with cut-out figures anyway. They have to be violent and quick, so a lot of the wholesale demolition you see in my films is forced on me.

'But there's another thing, I think. Like many of the *Monty Python* sketches, my cartoons come out of frustration. Living in the real world is a terrible thing. You think if you're reasonably nice to people, they'll be reasonably nice back. It doesn't work out like that – there's always a great big boot ready to come and squash you flat.

'Have you noticed how many of the *Monty Python* sketches are about people destroying other people? Or about one man reducing another to a gibbering idiot?

'John Cleese, you know, thinks he's on the side of the underdog, but he's not.

So how did a nice quiet, one might almost say shy, American get involved with them in the first place? 'Well, I met John Cleese when he was in New York with the revue *Cambridge Circus*' (Gilliam was then working as editor of *Help*, a stable-mate as one might have guessed of *Mad*).

'I was thinking of quitting the States anyway. I'd got fed up with it. That was five years ago when there seemed to be only the choice between getting wrapped up in the student revolutionary movement, or getting out of the country. I could see the cops were getting very nasty, so I got out.

'ANYWAY, I guess that I would have made a pretty heavy-handed revolutionary.'

Had he, then, thought of producing political cartoons?

'No!

'People think I do already because I use political characters in my films. But I *don't* do political cartoons.

'If I did, I'm sure I'd turn out like your average zealot, shouting all the time and nobody listening. That's pie-in-the-face time, isn't it?'

RADIO TIMES DATED 12 OCTOBER 197

In an interview to herald the start of series three, animator Terry Gilliam was asked where he got his inspiration from. After answering with a cartoon, he spoke some actual words...

Artist Terry Gilliam at home: 'My cartoons come out of frustration. Living in the real world is terrible. You think if you're reasonably nice to people, they'll be reasonably nice back. But there is always a great big boot ready to come and squash you flat'

RADIO TIMES DATED 12 OCTOBER 1972

EPISODE 13

FIRST TRANSMISSION
Thursday 18 January 1973
10.15pm BBC1

An overemotional Dickie Attenborough (Idle, above) hosts the **Light Entertainment Awards**; in London, 1895, a battle of wits between **Oscar Wilde** and James McNeill Whistler ends in a tight spot for George Bernard Shaw ("What I meant, Your Majesty..."); Pasolini is grilled over his new film, The Third Test Match; a brain salesman visits Mrs Zambesi; and a **Blood Donor** presents the doctor with stolen blood. Cameras are at Redcar for **International Wife-Swapping**, and Cleese makes his final appearance in *Flying Circus* – in bed with Palin.

Elvis, George and Brian

Monty Python boasts countless famous fans. Eric Idle found it "mind-blowing" to discover that among them was his teenage hero, Elvis Presley. Idle learnt that the King had all the tapes of the TV series, and he and his girlfriend in the mid-70s, actress Linda Thompson, would mimic the Pepperpot voices.

Beatles John Lennon and George Harrison were among other high-profile aficionados, the latter proving so influential that when finances were pulled on *The Life of Brian* just before shooting was due to start in 1978, Harrison (right) stumped up the necessaries by forming the company HandMade Films.

"The very fact that he made the film possible was extraordinary," says Eric Idle today. "I mean, I didn't think

he had that amount of money. He got about four and a half million dollars plonked down on the movie! Imagine trying to break that to the wife: 'I've just mortgaged the house and I'm going to make a Python movie.' 'Oh, that's a good idea, you mean the movie that nobody else would make?' [laughs] It still wouldn't have been made, to this day, but for him."

SERIES

4

1974

EPISODE

FIRST TRANSMISSION

Thursday 31 October 1974
9pm BBC2

Acknowledging, perhaps, that they
were no longer the full Monty without
Cleese, the team dropped the *Flying
Circus* from the title for this final,
foreshortened series. In every other
way, however, this is surrealist business
as usual. **The Golden Age
of Ballooning** celebrates the
pioneering work of the historically aware
Montgolfier Brothers
(left), who are paid a visit by a very
Glaswegian sounding **Louis XIV**
(right). Cases of mistaken identity
continue in the court of **George III**,
which is entertained by the Ronettes
(played by the Flirtations). Their song,
George III, was composed by Neil Innes
who, while uncredited in this episode,
plays more of a role in the Python story
from now on – on stage, in the films, and
in collaboration with Eric Idle on
Rutland Weekend Television.

LONDON   BBC Radio London
26 October–1 November 1974   Price 8p

Radio Times

Python's flying

Were the Montgolfier brothers the first balloonists? Was Louis XIV a Glaswegian? Should you vote Norwegian at the next election? Answers to these and other silly questions in Monty Python, Thursday BBC2 Colour Page 6: Who are these people, anyway?

Terry Gilliam created this cover for *Radio Times* (see letters, page 79). Asked what series four was about, Graham Chapman replied, mysteriously, "Concato's disease is, in fact, polyserositis."

Page 6

Now for something entirely similar

Cover Story Pull up your comfy chair! Switch on the telly! Cover the screen with the budgie's night curtain! They're back! The zany, anarchic, subversive etc etc *Python* returns as anarchic, subversive etc etc as ever, on Thursday. **Russell Miller** reveals the story of the men behind the madness

Monty Python
Thursday 9.0 pm
BBC2 Colour

THIS WEEK Monty Python takes to the air with a moving historical study entitled 'The Golden Age of Ballooning,' interspersed with a party political broadcast on behalf of the Norwegian Party.

No one will be watching the show with more interest than the writers and performers: Graham Chapman, Terry Gilliam, Terry Jones, Eric Idle and Mike Palin. If previous experience is anything to go by, they will all be laughing immoderately at their antics, for it is a cornerstone of *Python* humour that the authors themselves think it is funny. Chapman has been known to fall off his chair while watching it.

I had a hunch that together they would have an effect on each other
BARRY TOOK

The new series is the first without John Cleese, he of the tombstone face. Physically and emotionally exhausted by the strain of too many silly walks, he wanted more opportunity to work independently. His is the first defection since the team was put together in 1969 at the instigation of BBCtv comedy adviser, Barry Took.

'I had been watching them in two commercial television shows,' Took explained. 'Chapman and Cleese were in *At Last, The 1948 Show* and Palin, Idle, Jones and Gilliam's graphics were in *Do Not Adjust Your Set*. At the time, I felt that television comedy was getting a bit flat-footed and I just had a hunch that by getting them together and giving them their heads they would have an effect on each other.'

In fact, with the exception of Gilliam, it was almost inevitable that, in the end, they should work together. All of them were at Oxford or Cambridge at the same time, along with people like Bill Oddie, Tim Brooke-Taylor and Graeme Garden, later to become better known as the Goodies. It was a vintage period for inventive and creative humour which has overshadowed all undergraduate revue ever since.

Spike showed us there was no need to think in terms of sketches
TERRY JONES

While the leading Oxbridge writer/performers were ostensibly studying for their degrees, few of them had any intention of pursuing careers outside entertainment. So this little nucleus of academics and qualified doctors and lawyers drifted quite naturally into the world of television and the theatre, their paths constantly criss-crossing via programmes like *The Frost Report*, *I'm Sorry, I'll Read That Again* and *Do Not Adjust Your Set*.

A genre had been established, but it was still limited by the strictures of traditional comedy: three-minute sketches, punch lines and quickies. It was Spike Milligan who showed them the way out of the rut. Terry Jones explains: 'Right at the beginning, while we were still trying to think of a format, Spike did a BBC2 series called Q5. He broke up the rigid forms of comedy and showed us there was no need to think in terms of sketches and punchlines.

'Watching those shows we suddenly realised we had been writing in complete clichés. What he was doing to comedy was amazing and so from that moment we started breaking out of the traps.'

It took them about two weeks to think of a title. 'Flying circus' came first and Mike Palin suggested it should be called 'Gwen Dibley's Flying Circus.' Gwen Dibley is a pianist who once played in an afternoon concert given by the Shropshire Townswomen's Guild and Mike thought it would be nice if she had her own television show. But then, after much agonising, someone said: 'What about Python?' and 'Monty' was immediately suggested as the first name.

Python humour has been variously described as insane, surreal, anarchic, subversive, disgusting, violent, anachronistic, sexually-obsessed, offensive and zany. They are more likely to describe it as silly.

'As soon as you start to try and analyse,' says Jones, 'ask why it works, why it doesn't work, you can't do it any more. The only reason for *Python* is to be funny. I suppose if you have a consistent outlook and point of view, your attitudes must come over even if you are writing nonsense, but there is certainly no conscious effort to put over a message.'

The *Python* team operates very much as a comedy commune. When they start work on a new series, all of them initially either generate ideas, working alone or in pairs. This material is offered up for consideration at rowdy production meetings, where a great deal is discarded or radically changed and new ideas injected. From these sessions the final scripts emerge.

As long as we are still laughing at rehearsals then it stays
IAN MACNAUGHTON

Producer Ian Macnaughton (who also produced Milligan's Q5 series) says: 'As long as we are still laughing during rehearsal then it stays. If we stop laughing, it gets cut.'

Python's compelling visual image owes much to the macabre, Magritte-like animated cartoons contributed by Terry Gilliam, the only non-Oxbridge member of the team. Gilliam, an American, has lived in Britain for seven years. He became involved with Oxbridge surreal comedy after meeting John Cleese.

His first contributions were to *Do Not Adjust Your Set* and a forgettable series called *We Have Ways of Making You Laugh*. They didn't, except for an amazing animated film by Gilliam linking all Jimmy Young's terrible puns.

Unlike other members of *Python*, Terry is pessimistic about the future. Success, he feels, is threatening the enthusiasm that they had in the early days.

'It's not quite as much fun as it used to be and that really worries me. What was nice at the beginning – and I think it really communicated – was that we were all really enjoying it. Now it is getting a bit like work. I'm sure everyone feels this, although they may not admit it.'

I think we have avoided the pitfall of comedians of wanting to be loved
GRAHAM CHAPMAN

Graham Chapman certainly doesn't admit it. A qualified doctor, he has never practised except recently when he acted as unit doctor during the filming of *Monty Python and the Holy Grail.* 'Actually,' he admitted, 'all I had to do was dispense contraceptive pills to the girls when they realised we were away five weeks instead of four.'

Despite the growth of the Monty Python industry into films, books and records, as well as television series, he still gets a great deal of pleasure out of being involved.

'I think we have avoided that pitfall of all comedians of wanting to be loved. In a sense we want to avoid popularity. All we are trying to do is to be funny.

'As far as the BBC is concerned I think we have been rather successful. They have given us a tin shed in the car park for a production office. Well, that's fine. If they thought we were better we would probably be lost.' ●

RADIO TIMES DATED 24 OCTOBER

"They were all great as women because they played them all differently. John was probably the least successful because, somehow, he was always still John in drag and didn't seem as comfortable. I'd say the most convincing was Eric. His ladies were usually very prim and proper, which he did very well."
CAROL CLEVELAND

The silly heroines of the new Python series, thinly disguised and looking pleased to be back: top left, Mike Palin, right, Eric Idle, front left, Terry Jones and, right, Graham Chapman who is known to have fallen from his chair while viewing Python sillinesses

RADIO TIMES DATED 24 OCTOBER 1974

EPISODE 4

FIRST TRANSMISSION
Thursday 21 November 1974
9pm BBC2

Hamlet is analysed by a string of sex-obsessed, **Bogus Psychiatrists** – even a computer, which a nurse (Cleveland) destroys with a bazooka; **Nationwide** examines the benefits of a comfortable chair with a report from Westminster Bridge (the kind of location filming you can't imagine happening today); a couple find the proximity of the woman's **Father-in-Law** off-putting; **Boxing Promoter** Mr Gabriello sews his prize fighter's head back on before inviting the press into the changing room; the Pepperpots go shopping – mainly for a **Piston Engine**; and live coverage comes from Epsom of the **Queen Victoria Handicap** – football pundit Jimmy Hill (left) guests in full queenly regalia.

HIT OR AMIS?

In 1972 André Previn told *RT*, "In all my travelling on whatever continent... I have never seen a programme so unfailingly hilarious," but by series four, Kingsley Amis (left) was not so unstinting in his praise...

EPISODE 5

FIRST TRANSMISSION
Thursday 28 November 1974
9pm BBC2

There is extensive location filming for this penultimate episode – a "feature-length" story written mostly by Palin and Jones – reminiscent at times of the anti-war satire *Dr Strangelove*. The mayor and council officials assemble in Ulverston Road for a **Postal Box Dedication** – a speech repeated in French and German; **Mr Neutron** (Chapman), the most dangerous man in the world, goes missing; and Washington-based anti-alien agency Feeble sends Teddy Salad to track him down. When that fails, the USA bombs everywhere they think Mr Neutron might be: Cairo, Bangkok, Harrow, Enfield... The final, prohibitively expensive scenes are described by Idle's "man from the *Radio Times*", who reads from the 31 October 1974 edition of the magazine (right). A post-credits **Conjuring Today** is brought to an abrupt end by police.

Preview by Kingsley Amis

Page 5

theoretically believing) that the earth is a speck of warmth in an infinity of cold, that that warmth depends on a complex of huge variable forces, should be awe-inspiring – at any rate for the duration of the programme.

● This is going to be a full week, so you must forgive me for taking off at a rather faster trot than

● I shall sit down to watch **Monty Python** (Thursday BBC2) with my usual feelings of hope and dread. At their best, the fellows can be funny in a way that gets as near complete originality as anything I know; at their non-best, they curl me up. They may be tired of being told that they too often go too far, but their best way of dealing with that would be to do something about it, like having someone say, 'Are you sure you aren't going too far?' now and then. The ideas and scripts are often funnier than the performances: you can go too far by being extravagantly deadpan as well as by grinning and mouthing and eye-rolling (and don't tell me that going too far is the *whole point*).

A man from the Radio Times

MICHAEL PALIN: 66 I'm sure there were things in there that didn't work as well as they ought to have done.
On the other hand they were all part of the mix and because everything referred to everything else during one show it was quite difficult to take one thing out without unravelling the whole show 99

JOHN CLEESE: 66 I don't spend my life watching old Python episodes. Most of the bad ones I've simply forgotten.
If you're in a sitcom the story carries you through, but in any kind of sketch show some are always going to be much better than others. And of course not everyone agrees what *they* are 99

TERRY JONES: 66 I'm sure one day people will say the Pythons weren't funny. It happens with Shakespeare. Tragedy survives better than comedy, but I think we have a few more years 99

ERIC IDLE: 66 I don't go, 'Oh, I wish I'd done that differently 50 years ago.' That would be a useless waste of time, wouldn't it? I think that whatever it was doing was kind of instinctive and coming out of a very strange place, and was nice because nobody had done it. I just think it was a nicely chaotic show 99

ORN

OF **DAVID ATTENBOROUGH**, GILLIAM SAYS,

66 I didn't realise until Netflix had the big premiere of his new show [in 2019] that David Attenborough had been in one of the top positions of the BBC and had said yes to Python. **He's now getting credit for being the guy who said yes to Python.** I didn't realise that at the time. This is great! 99

EPISODE 6

FIRST TRANSMISSION
Thursday 5 December 1974
9pm BBC2

We meet the Garibaldis, taking part in the **Most Awful Family in Britain** competition (a sketch co-written by Chapman and Neil Innes): as the kitchen falls down around their ears, Gilliam's Kevin scoffs baked beans while lying on the sofa; a patient staggers into his GP's after being stabbed by the nurse; there's an awkward exchange between **the Brigadier and the Bishop**; Mrs Long Name is visited by **The Man Who Finishes Other People's Sentences**; and a profusely sweating David Attenborough (left) discovers the **Walking Tree of Dahomey**. Innes wrote an Appeal on Behalf of Extremely Rich People ("Graham performed it beautifully, I thought," says Innes). Among the other credited writers is Douglas Adams, who would go on to find fame with *The Hitchhiker's Guide to the Galaxy*.

Innes Own Right

Neil Innes joined *Flying Circus* for the fourth and final series, but his links with Python go back to ITV's *Do Not Adjust Your Set* (1967–9) when he was part of the Bonzo Dog Doo-Dah Band. "Yes indeed," he tells *RT* today, "the Bonzos, Eric, Michael and Terry G, Denise Coffey and David Jason were thrown together by [comedy executive] Humphrey Barclay – we were all aged about 12!"

So was he a fan of Python before he entered the fold? "*Flying Circus* came a little later in the scheme of things. The Bonzos went to America in 1969, so I didn't see much of the first series, but loved the ones I saw."

Innes's gifts as a solo songwriter really came to the fore in his *Circus* contributions, but also on stage with the Pythons and in *The Holy Grail*. Idle picked up on this when he was recruiting for *Rutland Weekend Television* and *The Rutles* (see page 86 onwards).

And the BBC wasn't slow in showing its appreciation, awarding Innes three series of his own song-and-comedy series, *The Innes Book of Records* (1979–81). Guests included John Betjeman reading a poem, Ralph Steadman drawing and Stanley Unwin quizzing himself on *Mastermind*. Innes himself, a former Norwich art student who said that he arrived in showbusiness by accident, played so many roles that the real Neil was scarcely visible.

"I liken what I do to plumbing sometimes," he told *RT* at the time. "I have a huge admiration for plumbers. I always think I could do what they do, but I invariably have to call one in and I am invariably impressed by what he does. I'd like people to think of my work in the same way."

AFTER THE CIRCUS

SOMETHING COMPLETELY DIFFERENT

RADIO, RUTLES & RAZZMATAZZ
ERIC IDLE

ther than animator Terry Gilliam, Eric Idle was the only Python to write material largely on his own, and before the *Flying Circus* came in to land for the final time, he went solo on the airwaves with *Eric Idle Presents Radio 5*. The show was broadcast on Radio 1 and featured Idle introducing records and performing sketches, playing nearly all the parts himself. Two series and nine episodes were broadcast between May 1973 and May 1974, plus a Christmas special in 1974. The second series also featured Idle's then wife Lyn Ashley, who had worked with the Pythons on a four-week sell-out residency at London's Drury Lane in spring 1974.

That stage production, and the albums recorded by Monty Python, showcased Idle's musical and lyrical gifts, which he would explore to even greater acclaim later on. It was the final, Cleese-less series of *Flying Circus* that persuaded Idle the time was right for something else: "I didn't like the six [episodes] without John. Everybody had

to be there. When John went missing it wasn't as good, so I said to Michael Palin, 'They offered us another seven [episodes] but I don't want to do another seven, it's not the same.' But what was good about that was that we then went on to writing movies, and John was happy to do that."

However, Idle's first project after *Flying Circus* was a TV sketch show focused on "Britain's smallest television network". As *Rutland Weekend Television* prepared to go live on BBC2 in May 1975, *Radio Times* spoke to its creator about a comedy "made on a shoestring budget" (see overleaf).

Asked today about *his* highlight from that show, collaborator Neil Innes tells *RT*: "Being dressed as an American sailor – along with choreographer Gillian Gregory – similarly garbed – and being abandoned by the film crew somewhere in

TOP OF THE WORLD

RT's Don Smith photographed Eric Idle on the roof of BBC Broadcasting House in central London in 1974 to publicise his show *Eric Idle Presents Radio 5*. But first he had to get past security (opposite, below)

Brighton. We had no money, nothing in our pockets. But thanks to a very friendly pub nearby, we had a couple of drinks and waited for the production team to find us."

Rutland Weekend Television also spawned pop pasticheurs the Rutles, whose eponymous TV comedy first aired on BBC2 on Easter Monday 1978. The film, a mockumentary that came out six years before *This Is Spinal Tap*, was written by and starred Idle as Dirk McQuickly, with songs written by his *RWT* colleague Neil Innes, who played Ron Nasty. South African musician Ricky Fataar and drummer John Halsey played the other members of the band, Stig O'Hara and Barry Wom (opposite right).

It was made in collaboration with members of the cult American show *Saturday Night Live*, including John Belushi, Dan Aykroyd and Bill Murray, and featured cameos from Beatle George Harrison as a TV reporter, plus Paul Simon and Mick Jagger playing themselves. "I'm proud of *The Rutles*," says Idle today. "I wrote it, so I'm very proud of it. It has a sort of nice naivety to it. It was a story that hadn't been told. Nobody had

❝ I'm proud of The Rutles. It has a sort of nice naivety to it ❞

Cover story From Pres B, the diminutive studio that gave you *Late Night* comes a show to tower over them all. Rutland Weekend Telev its writer and leading performer Eric Idle its ambitions will be as big reports on a meeting with Eric; and cartoonist **Bill Tidy** gives his impress

The tiniest show

Rutland Weekend Television
Monday BBC2 Colour

'"QUIPPED Eric Idle",' quipped Eric Idle. 'And that's why I don't often give quipping interviews.'

To be interviewed, according to Eric Idle, is to be misunderstood, and like all the good laughmakers Eric Idle does not easily allow himself to be misunderstood. To be misunderstood is to be open to attack.

'A comedian must never be vulnerable,' he said from above a struggling beard (soon to be shaved off) and from under the rebellious hair that is the despair of the BBC's energetic make-up department, who dash around cramming him into the wigs he uses for all his impersonations. 'The great comedians are always apparently invulnerable on stage although off stage they were not such supermen.'

During the days of *Monty Python*, when Eric was only several bright feet of a brilliant centipede, it was easy for him to melt into a crowd but from this week he is about to stand tall with new friends and a new comedy series called **Rutland Weekend Television**. Technically, it is a Presentation show and not Light Entertainment: 'It was made on a shoestring budget,' said Eric, 'and someone else was wearing the shoe.'

'Pres B,' the diminutive

Didn't he do . . . er, i very own General

Four bleats to the baa: the massed sheep of Rutland join in the choruses in RWT's own entry for th Eurovision Song Contest

Match of the Day ment of the one an

RADIO TIMES DATED 8 MAY 1975

Radio Times

Here is the cheap news

. . . from low-budget
Rutland Weekend Television,
Monday BBC2 Colour
— and this is Eric Idle reading it
Page 9: The tiniest show on TV

RWT

IT'S A SMALL WORLD

Eric Idle's first post-*Circus* TV show, *Rutland Weekend Television*, made it on to the cover of *Radio Times* in the issue of 10 May 1975. The two-page feature inside included illustrations from esteemed cartoonist Bill Tidy. "It was made on a shoestring budget and someone else was wearing the shoe," said Idle of *RWT*

ight and *Up Sunday*, e and in the hands of d itself. **Irma Kurtz** TV station's output

nTV

Centre. 'The studio is ne size as the weather t studio,' Eric said, g his blue, blue eyes the cigarettes he s and is always encour- other people to give up, early as good.'

B may be small but its on history is large: the d space has been home ne-Up, *The Book Pro- e, Film Night, The End Pier Show* and *Up Sun- One* presenter can sit in a small studio like and the atmosphere is but when several active sters like Eric and his want to use the same for a comic showdown, estricted area becomes matical. For ➤➤ **11**

RWT combines the excite- ne other – and saves money

---

9 ◀◀◀ example, sets had rare- ly been used before in Pres B and getting them up there was a bit like swinging a cat in a coal cellar – except the cat loved it.

'We had to bring the sets up four floors for each scene, then take them down again. While the next set was coming up, we'd change our make-up. Every minute mattered. It's not always funny to be funny from ten in the morning until ten at night.

'As for ad-libbing, what ad- libbing? You don't ad-lib when you're working with three cameras and anyway the material goes out months after you've made it.'

Eric, whose book *Hello Sailor* was published in March, is at least half a writer and like most writers at least half a loner; he is a loner however who works well with good mates. Although *Rutland Weekend Television* (whether the title was originally his idea or John Cleese's he isn't honestly sure) was worked out at his isolated home in France which he shares with his wife Lyn and his young son Cary,

There's no outdoor filming, no costly costumes in RWT's plays

he is not stingy about his debt to colleagues.

'Neil Innes is superb. I must be his biggest fan. Henry Woolf played Toulouse-Lautrec in the West End. He's the best small philosopher in London at the moment. And David Battley – what can I say? Straight, pale, dead-pan and brilliant. Our cameraman, Peter Bart-

RWT's window on our world; one version of Panorama *that does not go abroad and saves on costly hospitality for studio guests*

RADIO TIMES DATED 8 MAY 1975

---

lett, filmed the Queen but says I'm easier to work with.'

Now 32, Eric drifted apolo- getically into the Cambridge *Footlights Revue*, then slid on to ITV's *At Last the 1948 Show* where he befriended Marty Feldman; Eric then played a major role in *Do Not Adjust Your Set*, involved himself innocently in *Twice a Fort- night*, bumped into David Frost and careered into *Monty Python's Flying Circus* with all the books, films and foreign tours that involved.

In the meantime, he scrib- bled at scripts and books between dawn and midday, avoided biting his nails and only started smoking cigarettes reluctantly, late in life. Al- though he can be silly when he wants to be, his surname is the only thing about him that doesn't make sense.

'And that's a quip,' quipped Eric.

'No one has had the courage to copy me'

'I DON'T BELIEVE in giving the public exactly what they want,' explains Neil Innes, whose bizarre blend of music and humour first flowered in the artistic hothouse of the now defunct Bonzo Dog Band dur- ing the late 60s. Having worked with Eric Idle on *Do Not Adjust Your Set* and the *Monty Python* LPs and stage shows, Innes now finds himself responsible for *Rutland Weekend's* music.

'On these shows I parody things that people take seri- ously,' he says. 'I suppose I'm doing what Hoffnung did for the classics, for music in gen- eral. Of course, as it's TV it would be daft to just sit and strum a guitar – so I like to add an unexpected, surreal visual aspect to jolly things along.'

Personal experience has left Innes with a poor opinion of stardom: 'It's bad for one's mental health, getting no peace, being chivvied around and having to keep up a facade.' So he finds plenty of targets to poke fun at in the world of pop. 'I don't like showbiz – what it does, or how it's presented – but I do like people; the trouble is that our society can't be much good if they need such cheap dreams to be thrown at them.'

But when it comes to dissect-

---

ing the dreams so glamorously portrayed on TV, Innes avoids vicious satire: 'I concentrate on the human aspect, like would-be pop idol Stoop Solo, the ballad singer with the con- ceited delivery and a "gorilla chest"' – the ultimate in virile body wigs. 'He's the epitome of the guys who go in for TV talent shows.

'Then there's the archetypal *Top of the Pops* film sequence of someone who has nothing to do with the record wander- ing around in a wood, or some- where equally idyllic. Well,

RWT's closedown poems are short – and out of copyright

we've got this very arty sequence of someone stumping up and down in a laundromat – it's what people really do, you see.

'Obviously visual tricks work better in a big studio,' adds Innes, 'but as *RWT* is sup- posed to be a duff local station it was all to the good. Mind you, the logistics of working in a place that size got quite complex – after all, you can't really get on with your protest singer sequence with half Nelson's flagship in there. It was quite batty.'

Batty or not, Innes finds that his florid imagination has be- gun to take on a life of its own. For instance, 'Big Boots,' his stilt-legged, ten-foot high, rock guitarist hero who is resurrec- ted on *RWT*, 'for old time's sake' – is not dissimilar to the Pinball Wizard outfit that Elton John wears in the Ken Russell film *Tommy*.

'Some people get like the Northern comics, back-stabbing over pinched material, but it just doesn't matter to me – it just makes me think of something else and go on my own surreal way. After all, no one has had the courage to copy me – wear- ing a duck on their head.' ●

---

mocked the story of the Beatles and it's nice when you find an area of new territory." Fellow Rutle Neil Innes is similarly enthusiastic: "*The Rutles* [pictured right] was a wonderful project. Everyone knew what to do. It's prob- ably the most fun thing I've ever been involved with."

The musical theme continued to reap dividends for Idle. *Always Look on the Bright Side of Life*, his song from the 1979 film *Life of Brian*, has become synonymous with Monty Python. And *Spamalot*, his musical based on their film *The Holy Grail*, became an all-singing, all-dancing

hit in the noughties with its surreal tale of King Arthur and the Knights of the Round Table: "We took what was a very fine and crazy film and made it into a Broadway musical, which worked and ran for five years," says Idle.

Little Britain's David Walliams caught up with his hero Eric Idle for *Radio Times* when *Spamalot* opened in London in 2006 (see overleaf).

Speaking to Radio Times today, Idle says he doesn't worry about whether *Flying Circus* has stood the test of time, or whether they should have done things differently. "Whatever it was doing, it was kind of instinctive and coming out of a very strange place, and it was nice because nobody had done it. We were the first into the new studio with the toys. There wasn't anybody who'd done it in colour. I think

Pete Cook and Dudley Moore had done a bit of it in black and white, Alan Bennett had done a series, but the BBC thoughtfully wiped most of the series that you could compare it to [laughs].

"It was a nicely chaotic show. No show has ever been run by the writers. Ever. And that's why it is good. Because we would rewrite a lot and pass it around. We were professional writers. We'd been doing it since we'd left college, professionally and on television – on *The Frost Report* and for various shows. And we weren't bad at performing because we'd done our own kids' show [*Do Not*

❝It used to annoy people and upset them – and I liked it better when we did that!❞

BUNNY BUSINESS
Eric Idle and David Walliams sport "Killer Rabbit" slippers promoting *Spamalot*

IDLE

Little Britain's **David Wall**
to seek his views on

What's it like being part of something as huge and influential as *Monty Python*? You're carrying around so much history, so much expectation.
But that's exactly what it is: history. In fact, it's been history since 1983. Obviously, we're all connected in a business sense, but all this talk about "You guys should get back together" is a complete load of b******s. And let's not forget that when we were together, there were actually lots and lots of people who f***ing hated us.

Do you still get on? Has the success of *Spamalot* [the Broadway musical based on the film *Monty Python and the Holy Grail* opening in the UK this week and profiled in *The South Bank Show*] brought you closer together?
The only thing that ever bonded us together was the work. To be honest, we weren't really interested in each other as people. Even when Graham [Chapman] became an alcoholic, I don't think any of us actually noticed. We were a bit like a great football team. Very different individuals, but stick us on the football field and we were fantastic.
Working on *Spamalot* did mean that I had to have meetings with the others

28

Adjust Your Set], *At Last the 1948 Show*... everybody had a lot of experience and was ready to go. It was very fortuitous."

So what is he proudest of? "It's an extraordinary thing. It went to something like 93 countries – you can't get your mind round something like that – and it was a number one in Japan! The good news is that everybody is silly in the world: they understand comedy and daftness. They have Silly Walks days in the Czech Republic... it's very strange but I think it's kind of healthy, it lets people loose a bit more.

"The disappointment to me now is that people like it and think it's rather cuddly and lovely, whereas it used to annoy people and upset them – and I liked it better when we did that! I think it was much more fun when it was *épater la bourgeoisie*. We got a lot of complaints from a certain section of the British public. And that was good. That meant it was current.

"I suppose the most amazing thing is it went to America and it changed American comedy. They just went nuts for it and it influenced a whole generation: *Saturday Night Live*, Chevy Chase, Robin Williams and Steve Martin, all of those people. All influenced by Python. And it made it possible for them to have crazy shows, which they didn't really have in America at all. It's why Gilliam had to come to England!"

ORSHIP

o to his hero, *Monty Python's* **Eric Idle**, , fame and hit musical *Spamalot*

veto on anything to sort of gentlemen's ke sure things don't don't get taken recorded some y on and it seemed m sure they're eques they've certainly am!

in LA, do you ritish comedy? ice – Ricky l comedy *The League of* re and I think guess it's comedy to was so close lly interests me the Pythons. nt. Billy e about Billy ensor. He'll ing. And

ust saying ass. We see

you on BBC America all the time and, believe me, America is a very big pond. Throw a stone in and the ripples can go a long way. That's why the whole f***ing country seems to know the entire script of *Holy Grail*.

Do you ever get lonely in LA?
You're kidding, right? I'm surrounded by beautiful women and I've been happily married for 30 years to Tania, a woman who used to appear in *Playboy*. My life is . . . unbelievable.

You probably have no memory of this but I did see you in a shop in LA a couple of years ago. I was desperate to talk to you, but I felt that the best thing I could do was give you a bit of space and let you carry on parading around the shop in the very colourful dressing gown you were buying.
I definitely remember the dressing gown. You should have come up and said something. I wouldn't have minded.

Have you ever wondered why the Americans "got" *Python*? It just seems so British.
There was only one reason why the ▷

◁ Americans watched us. Tits! OK, they were cutout, cardboard, cartoon Victorian tits, but when you're a young college kid, you have to take what you can get. When we first went to the States, they did actually say, "We love you guys, you're just like Benny Hill."
The whole success of *Python* was bizarre and totally unplanned. It went

the f**k was that all about?" It was just this show that we did, but it keeps on going and going. It never stops. George Harrison really helped me deal with it. Look at what he went through, but at the end of it all, he asked himself, "What is the point of fame and success?" And you know what? It has no point at all.

"It was just this show that we did, but it keeps on going. It never stops"

to 70 countries! What did the French make of us? What did the Japanese make of us? That level of attention is very difficult to understand, and it took a lot of therapy to help me crawl out of it.

Did it scare you?
Absolutely. Your first instinct is to run to the hills. Even when it was over, I used to think, "What

You and George became mates very early on, didn't you?
He was an easy man to get on with. I remember sitting with him on a film set once, feeling a bit dejected because Michael Palin and John Cleese were getting all the good scenes. I said, "I never get a look-in when those two are around." He just said, very dryly, "You should try being in a band with Lennon and McCartney." I thought to myself, "Yeah . . . point taken."

I've read that you're also into Buddhism. Did that come from George, too?
The Buddhism thing is just my little reminder of the billions of people on this planet who are all praying and all claiming to worship the one and only true faith. I don't have beliefs. I think beliefs are b******s. Look at the trouble they cause.

Is it fair to say that both *Python* and *Spamalot* came out of very difficult political times?
There's some truth in that. In the 60s and 70s, there was all sorts of s**t going

SAY NO MORE! David performs his Sebastian from *Little Britain* routine on Eric

on, but then we came along dressing up as women and being very surreal. Now you've got America in turmoil and a whole country in despair, but we come along with the Knights Who Say Ni [in *Spamalot*]. Comedy is cathartic. Always has been. The Goons came out of the Second World War; the Fringe came out of all those dark years of Tory government. Unfortunately, some comedians tend to forget the real value of making people laugh. Making people laugh isn't easy.

When did you realise it was something that you could do?
We all know that comedy is about getting laid and, yes, before you ask, we all did very well, thank you. Mind you, I think Jonesy [Terry Jones] had the most sex out of all of us. As for the first time I thought about making people laugh . . . probably at boarding school. There was a lot of bullying going on and if you could make someone laugh just as they were going to punch you, there was more chance you'd get away. John Cleese reckoned that comedy is all about saying, "You can only laugh at me when I tell you." Comedy is a defence.

I once saw John Cleese and wanted to go up and say "hello", but he looked quite scary.
John is very scary. Michael on the other hand is very, very nice. A very, very nice man. Too nice, sometimes. He hates upsetting people.

How did it feel when you all got back together for the Broadway opening of *Spamalot* last year?
We missed Chapman, of course, but it was fantastic. I felt immensely proud. I remember thinking, "The next time we're all going to be in the same room is when another one of us dies." We've decided that we're going to die alphabetically. Chapman went first . . . it's not hard to work out who's going to be next.

Monty Python's Spamalot opens at the Palace Theatre, London, on 16 October.

LINKS
www.southbankshow.com

ERIC THE CV
Just some of Idle's not-so-idle moments

1943 Born in South Shields, Tyne and Wear.
1965 Elected Footlights president at Cambridge University, succeeding Graeme Garden.
1966 Becomes a writer on satirical TV show *The Frost Report*.
1967 Co-writes and appears on *Do Not Adjust Your Set*, joining future fellow Pythons Michael Palin, Terry Jones and Terry Gilliam.
1969 *Monty Python's Flying Circus* (right) makes its debut on BBC1 – comedy is never the same again.
1971 Is one of an army of writers for *The Two Ronnies*.
1975 *Monty Python and the Holy Grail* is released at cinemas.
1975 Idle's first post-Python project, *Rutland Weekend Television*, airs, leading to music spoof *The Rutles: All You Need is Cash* in 1978.
1976 Appears on America's *Saturday Night Live* show.
1979 *Monty Python's Life of Brian* opens to huge controversy.
1983 *Monty Python's The Meaning of Life* premieres: it's the team's final film.
1990 Sings the theme tune to *One Foot in the Grave*.
1991 His song *Always Look on the Bright Side of Life* makes number three in the charts.
2003 "Appears" in *The Simpsons*.
2005 *Spamalot* (below) opens on Broadway to great acclaim.

MARK HARRISON / WITH THANKS TO THE SAVOY HOTEL

**hile they** were creating sketches for *Flying Circus*, Michael Palin wrote with Terry Jones, so it was no surprise when the two joined forces for their next major TV project. Looking back today, Palin recalls: "Terry Hughes the producer came up to me and said he wanted to do something with me. And I said I'd like to do some comedy, but we had to be very careful to make sure it was unlike Python, or son of Python – all that – and I wanted to work on the writing of it with Terry Jones."

One thing that aided the transition was the fact that later episodes of *Flying Circus* contained more elaborate storylines. Palin explains: "The idea of long-form sketch or even a half-hour show was always something that was in the back of our minds – Terry Jones and myself – I'm not sure about the others as much, but we enjoyed storytelling and we felt that was the way to go: to make each episode a story.

"Of course, it wasn't always right for Python, because everyone was writing different bits. But there was one episode, *The Cycling Tour* [see page 63], which was important, because it was one whole story. The other Pythons seemed to be very happy with that."

So Palin and Jones created a one-off comedy, entitled *Tomkinson's Schooldays*, with Palin in the lead and Jones in a guest role, and it aired in January 1976. When that later became the first of a six-part series in September 1977, called *Ripping Yarns*, *Radio Times* was there to open the book on the whole adventure…

RIPPING YARNS AND TRAVEL TALES
MICHAEL PALIN

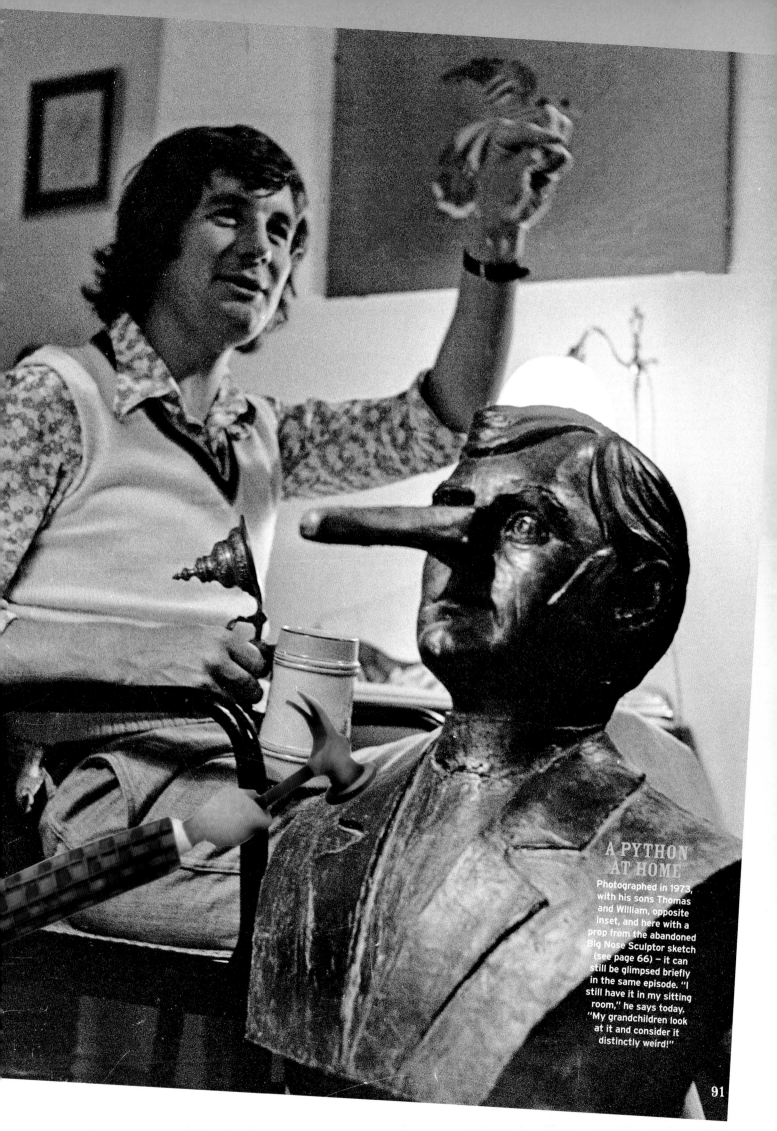

Comedy

This week's episode of the new series *Ripping Yarns* is called *The Testing of Eric Olthwaite*: 'a boy becomes a man in the harsh world of the Depression'. In a series in which wit is a goad to be used on sacred cows Michael Palin and Terry Jones have taken every parodist's liberty with English literature. Who is this Michael Palin? When was this streak of lunacy allowed to intrude upon a predictable career leading from public school to advertising agency?

RIPPING YARNS

MIKE PALIN is the fresh faced, nice looking one, the only member of the *Monty Python* team you can imagine appealing to a middle-class mum – except, that is, when he is going through his famous gay lumberjack routine or impersonating Hitler. With his neat, short hair and his winning smile he looks a little like the successful advertising executive his parents once wanted him to become.

'They wanted me to go into something *sound*. I remember the name Courtauld's being mentioned, and there was the usual careers master who

Birkdale Preparatory School, Sheffield. June, 1952.

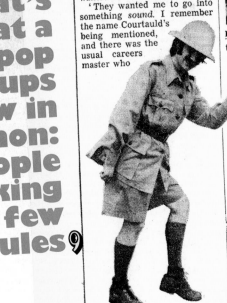

SHREWSBURY SCHOOL. May, 1959.

Palin's education was conventional: Sheffield prep school, Shrewsbury

6 **That's what a lot of pop groups saw in Python: people breaking a few rules** 9

twitched and told you you had to go into glass because he had 20 free Pilkington brochures stuffed in his desk. But we agreed on advertising.' Advertising was the only thing they could think of which was creative but sound with it. In the event, of course, he became a comic, an actor, and a writer, which is creative enough but only sound if you're lucky and good. Palin has turned out to be both.

Unlike any other member of his family he is qualified to play cricket for Yorkshire (a useless qualification since, although being a prodigious thrower of the cricket ball at prep school, he gave the game up when he went to Shrewsbury). Mr and Mrs Palin were Southerners living in Sheffield, where Mr Palin was the export manager of a steel company, and their son Michael was born in 1943. 'The war

came to an end shortly afterwards and there was no chance to go down the air-raid shelter built at vast expense.' He conveys the impression that his nativity and the cessation of hostilities were cause and effect. 'The Germans didn't bomb Sheffield much after I was born.'

Beside Tomkinson's, whose schooldays were the basis of the first of his series *Ripping Yarns*, the Palin education was conventional, even mundane. The prep school was Birkdale, Sheffield, from which he slipped away as often as possible to sample the delights of the new 3-D effect in the local cinema. 'I didn't get bashed up in the playground,' he admits, shamefacedly, and when he went on to the same public school as his father he discovered an aptitude for 'being consistently good at being second'. This culminated in a spell as 'Vice-Head of House' where he first learned to e...

power without responsibility. Shrewsbury, of course, enjoys a notoriety as a breeding ground for satirists, who tend to gravitate towards *Private Eye*, which at times has been a sort of Alternative Old Salopian Magazine. Palin did not take to satire, though he did write short poems for the school magazine. These were serious. 'Unfortunately you couldn't just sit and read a book in the afternoon. That was right out.' Instead he began rowing. 'It was very unpleasant at first. You had a fixed seat so you got nothing but blisters on the bum.' Later on, he graduated to a moving seat, a blisterless bum and, true to form, a place in the school secon... eight. It became fun.

Acting was a virtually illic... pleasure since it conflicted wi... work. He turned down a b... part in *The Applecart*, taking smaller one instead so that h... parents wouldn't notice he w... actually in it. His father, claims, slept through all h... lines and never realised.

Part of the parental ambiti... was the desire to model his ed... cation precisely on his father... but his capacity for second be... meant that he failed the e... trance to Clare, Cambrid... and had to make do with Bra... nose, Oxford – a second best... which he rema... deeply grate... 'BNC's like a r... way waiti... room,' he sa... 'anyone can... in.' But be... going up, got his... big break... had... months... kill, but... stead o... ing to... occo or b... an *au pa*... the Y... like ever... else, I... and worke... the pub... departmen... the steelw... This was... have bee... first st... the road to white-...

In 1979, after *Ripping Yarns*, Palin went solo for a Radio 1 programme in which different celebrities were given the chance to take on the role of DJ. *RT* spoke to him then, and Palin recalled the first time he heard Elvis on the radio, when *Heartbreak Hotel* "arrived like a thunderbolt on *Family Favourites*. It demanded a very strong response one way or the other, which I think is a good thing in any form of entertainment. In a sense, *Monty Python* did the same thing – people either loathed it or loved it, and that's what Elvis did for me.

"Doing comedy, in a sense, has always provided its own release. Python in particular put us in a position of being able to write what we felt about what was going on around us, the people we saw and the attitudes we wanted to criticise – it was our equivalent of the Who writing *My Generation* and people going along to their concerts, shaking their fists and smoking pot. And I think that is

SPINNING A YARN

Radio Times devoted two pages to *Ripping Yarns* in its 27 September 1977 edition, with co-creator Michael Palin retracing the threads of his comedy career. Making each other laugh at Oxford, he and a friend, Robe... Hewison, decided: "It was more sensible t... make money telling jokes to other people instead of each other"

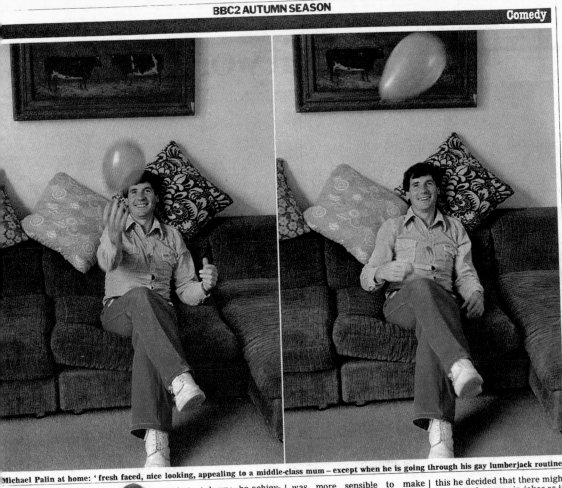

Michael Palin at home: ' fresh faced, nice looking, appealing to a middle-class mum – except when he is going through his gay lumberjack routine '

success in the advertising industry but, alas for such aspirations, the young Palin fell in with a group of strolling Thespians who were known as The Brightside and Car-brook Co-operative Players.

He was the juv-enile lead in a drama about sev-en people waiting to be shot at dawn: he achiev-ed one of the great moments of his career with a super-real-istic artificial scar on one arm, guaranteed to shock and stun the most hardened audience; there was even an award at a drama festi-val in Huddersfield. A star was born.

Imbued with a taste for bright lights and greasepaint, the first thing he did at Oxford was trot round to the Dramatic So-ciety and land a key role as a second peasant in the next major production. Third peasant was another BNC undergraduate named Robert Hewison. ' We got talking,' says Palin. And be-fore long they got telling jokes too. Miraculously they dis-covered that when they did that they spent a lot of time laughing. When they stop-ped they decided that ' it was more sensible to make money telling jokes to other people instead of each other '.

Whereupon they set up as ' Seedy Entertainers ' and were hired to perform at the Christ-mas party of the Oxford Uni-versity Psychological Society. The psychologists laughed too and the Palin-Hewison act be-came the star cabaret turn of their Oxford year. Those of us interested in spotting future success immediately jotted them down as the Dud and Pete of their generation and are now mildly frustrated by Hewison's copping out of humour to write serious books about Ruskin and literary London in the war.

Palin's career has suffered no such deflections. At Oxford he won a respectable second-class degree after writing an essay on Hegel based entirely on read-ing about him, for the first time, on the bus taking him to the examination schools. Despite this he decided that there might be as much money in jokes as in advertising and ever since he has let himself be assimilated gracefully and easily into the lucrative world of graduate humour so nearly monopolised by Oxbridge people.

To see him sitting in his glassy eyrie, constructed *House and Garden*-like on the roof of his house in Gospel Oak, one almost, perish the thought, feels one is interviewing an ex-tremely successful executive from J. Walter Thompson or McCann-Erickson. He's just bought the house next door to provide more room for his three attractive children and his wife, Helen. It's difficult to think of him as a gay lumberjack. In fact, I'd say he was a credit to Shrews-bury, Oxford, and Mr and Mrs Palin.

what a lot of pop groups saw in Python – people sticking their necks out a bit and breaking a few rules. They were doing it through music and we did it through laughter, but the two may be more similar than one thinks."

Palin returned to his *Comic Roots* for a BBC1 documentary, in 1983. On that occa-sion, aged 40, he thought of himself as per-manently 20… "Though at 20 I was probably much more serious, thinking there was a great world out there and one should go and do respectable things in it. Now I feel free to be rather sillier."

Yet he insisted that "Just because I can't take things seriously for very long, it doesn't mean that I don't want to be taken seriously at times… But I can use humour as a defence against the monstrous things in the world, just as I did to avoid getting bashed up at school."

Living happily with his wife Helen and their three children in the same unpretentious house in north-west London that they had occupied since 1968, Palin told *RT*, "This is where I am, and where I've been for a long time: and staying here is what I feel success is all about."

Though the Pythons by this stage all had their own independent projects, Palin explained that even on a joint one they worked separately, sometimes resolving whole sketches on their own before pre-senting them to the group – "a nerve-rack-ing thing. I always think, 'Perhaps it's not going to work this time and

Michael Palin, EX-PYTHON

THE LIFE OF MICHAEL

In 2006, the publication of the first volume of his *Diaries* (which became Radio 4's *Book of the Week*) gave us the perfect excuse for a natter with the genial Mr Palin for the 7 October edition of *Radio Times*

As his diaries from the late 1960s and 1970s are published, **Michael Palin** explains why he's still laughing at his old jokes

Would you ever rule out a *Monty Python* reunion?

Well, to be pedantic, we can't ever properly re-unite, because Graham [Chapman] is dead, and *Monty Python* was all about that mix of six different performers. That said, I wouldn't mind us working together again, because my fellow Pythons are still the people who make me laugh most in the whole world.

What's your favourite sketch?

People usually quote the Dead Parrot sketch, or the Spanish Inquisition, or Nudge Nudge, but personally I've always fought a rearguard action for the Fish-slapping Dance [pictured below]. Firstly, there's the physical disparity between me and John [Cleese]; then there's the idea of the small man (ie me) irritating the large man (him) by slapping him with little pilchards. The bit I love, though, is where John takes hold of a big fish and then goes through a certain amount of ceremonial fish drill – pausing, taking aim – before whacking me with it

PILCHARDS ON PARADE
John Cleese has the last laugh as Michael Palin hits the water

and knocking me into the Thames. I'm told Japanese tourists still visit the spot where the sketch was filmed.

What were the strongest reactions your work provoked?

When we did stage shows in the UK, groups of people would wear knotted hankies on their heads and book the front row. But it was in the USA that the reception was the most intense. I think *Python* was something the college-educated young had been waiting for. It was irreverent, inconsequential and silly, and those are just not things that America does.

You've been filming recently in the Baltic and

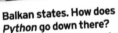

Balkan states. How does *Python* go down there?

As it happens, it's extremely popular in the countries that make up the former Yugoslavia. Because their Communist regime, under Tito, was more liberal than others, they were allowed to watch Western programmes on TV, and (I'm told) loved the fact that on *Monty Python* we kicked the shins of authority. It allowed them if not to express rebellion openly, at least to enjoy watching others do it.

Do you still find the sketches funny?

I went to a 20th anniversary screening of *Life of Brian* at the Odeon Leicester Square, with John and the two Terries (Jones and Gilliam), and all of us roared with laughter! Heaven knows what people thought of us! But we wrote all that material to make ourselves laugh, so I suppose it's a good thing that it still does. I'm

quite proud of it; even 35 years later, *Python* still fills a need!

How different are you now from the person you were then?

Oh, not very different at all, really. What has changed is that I don't now suffer from the same anxieties as I did then. The thing about *Monty Python* is that it was very stop-start, very uncertain – at any one time there was always at least one person who didn't want to carry on, or who didn't want to do another series.

Finally, how did you describe yourself on your passport?

"Actor". I used to put "writer", but some countries interpreted that as "journalist", ie trouble! Once I was going on holiday with the family to Sierra Leone, and we were told the day before our departure that they had all been given visas, but I'd been refused. I don't think my family minded, but I was a bit put out!

Christopher Middleton

Michael Palin reads from his *Diaries 1969–79: the Python Years* on *Book of the Week*, weekdays on Radio 4. There are also two Python-related documentaries on Saturday BBC2: *It's… the Monty Python Story*; and *Omnibus – Life of Python*.

EYEVINE

23

I'll be met with stunned embarrassment.'

"I don't think there's a comedian anywhere who knows for sure that something will be funny before he hears people laugh. Every time you've got to establish this moment of contact, and hear this direct reaction – this actual physical sound being emitted from people's throats."

He admitted that the more serious and solitary part of him longed to go off and write something he can completely control, like a novel or a travel book. But when you find you can elicit that elusive sound from the throat, "it becomes like a drug, and you can never totally turn your back on it".

After appearing in a series of acclaimed films in the 1980s, including Terry Gilliam's *Brazil* and John Cleese's *A Fish Called Wanda* (the latter winning Baftas for both Cleese and Palin), he wrote and presented the series *Around the World in 80 Days* in 1989 ("The best decision I ever made"), the first of several hugely popular BBC travelogues and books for which he became famous all over again.

He also got to indulge his passion for trainspotting in *Great Railway Journeys*, travelling through England and Scotland in 1980 and around Ireland, from Derry to Kerry, in 1994.

ur interview with him in 1995 saw Palin in a more reflective mood. "The Pythons," he said, "were lucky because we were allowed to let our imaginations run riot and were paid for indulging our subconscious. It was like group therapy. We made various connections we wouldn't have dared on our own."

Reacting to being known as the "normal" Python, he added, "That's like being called the less violent of the Kray twins. That dread word 'normal'. There's a little bit of madness in me, I'm glad to say. It's prevented me doing responsible things, like being head of house at school or working in a bank. It's why I've been able to earn my living as a writer for 30 years."

As for the raising of his profile, he said, "People identify with me since the travels. It's not something I set out to achieve, but it's part of the appeal. I'm not some remote star figure. I'm a person who gets dirty on shows."

GOING LOCO

Palin rode the rails for *Great Railway Journeys* and, below, in Sudan for *Pole to Pole* in 1992

On top of the world: Palin crossing the Nubian desert, Sudan, on his way from *Pole to Pole*

'The Pythons were lucky because we were paid for indulging our subconscious. It was like group therapy'

Completely different: Palin (right) with the Python team in 1969

Having then just published his first novel, *Hemingway's Chair*, Palin had an uncharacteristic outburst of self-praise. "It's good," he said. "I've done modesty. People didn't believe it because they think I'm just trying to be nice. Working is my therapy and keeps me sane. It does me good to have a bit of shock treatment now and again, to try to become a playwright, a novelist, or travel to a part of the world I've never seen. Varying my daily routine keeps my mind reasonably clear and fresh."

While we were putting together this *Monty Python at 50* bookazine, Palin was knighted for services to travel, culture and geography, which he says was a great surprise. "I really wasn't sure which way to go with it," he tells *RT*. "I thought, well, I've been two knights. I've been Sir Galahad and I've been the Knight who said Ni, and here's the real thing!" Have the other Pythons teased him about it? "No," he laughs, "they've been remarkably understanding about it, really. I was expecting a lot more leg-pulling. They're obviously softening up a bit as we get older."

an Sir Michael sum up what inspired him about belonging to the world-famous comedy collective? "Python certainly stretched me as a performer and as a writer," he says. "That's what I'm very grateful to Python for.

"We had a wonderful cast and even if you weren't doing something yourself, you could write for somebody else who would do it wonderfully. It was that feeling of being a self-contained group – sometimes I suppose others would see it as rather arrogantly closed, but it was really us against the rest of the world.

"We wanted to produce our own material, we wanted to be in there writing it, performing it, choosing the locations, financing it... And I realised that's very important. I'm quite easy-going and I probably would have been talked out of things that the other Pythons were strong enough to fight for, so it was that feeling of being together, fighting for what we wanted to do in the way that we wanted to do it.

"At the time, there would be a focus group here and a study group there, or some executive from the BBC would tell us how it ought to be, and they never ever got it right. No, honestly! No one ever got it right.

"There was a lovely man called Michael White who financed most of *Holy Grail* and yet, at one of the viewings, he just said the Black Knight fight had got to go: 'It's unpleasant, it's violent, no one wants to see that sort of thing...' And of course it's now one of the most popular Python sketches ever.

"So 'stand up for what you feel is right' – that was the strength of Python. That was the inspiration I got in later work: if you've got a good idea, fight for it, you know, don't be talked out of it. But if it's a bad idea, that's your fault!"

'Stand up for what you feel is right – that was the strength of Python'

95

SHERLOCK, BASIL AND BOND JOHN CLEESE

In early 1973, Cleese broke free of the Python camp, starring as Sherlock Holmes in a BBC *Comedy Playhouse* entitled *Elementary My Dear Watson*, along with Willie Rushton, Bill Maynard, Josephine Tewson and John Wells.

"Dear Bill Maynard, he died recently, I thought he was wonderful," Cleese says today of his Holmesian affair. "One of the great comedy actors, people don't tend to remember him, but he was just lovely. And I also met a wonderful Scottish comic called Chic Murray... some great old pros. But it was quite a bizarre script because it was written by NF Simpson, who had a brief spell as a very noticed playwright who wrote *One Way Pendulum* and *A Resounding Tinkle*. That was a very good experience, I liked the director [Harold Snoad] and I loved Willie Rushton. Lovely man. Played cricket with him."

But it was while filming *Elementary My Dear Watson* that Cleese confided to *Radio Times*: "It's all this hanging around I can't stand. Seventy-five per cent of *Python* is spent hanging around doing extra work. I hung about for three hours in a Tudor costume, tights, the lot, when only my right forearm was in shot, although they reassured me that connoisseurs would know it was John Cleese's forearm." As it transpired, the *Comedy Playhouse* aired on the same night as the final episode of *Flying Circus* that he appeared in.

As he tells *RT* now: "I said I thought we were repeating ourselves and I was very keen to go off and write something with Connie [Booth], my wife. Because I've always been decades ahead of the rest of the world, I realised how important it was to have women there as co-writers, so I was one of the very first to do that!"

While Monty *Python's Flying Circus* was on the air between 1969 and 1974, John Cleese's mind was already starting to drift elsewhere. The seeds of a future smash were sown while the troupe were on location in Paignton, Devon, in May 1970. Staying at a hotel in nearby Torquay, Cleese was intrigued by the rude behaviour of its owner...

In the early 1970s, Cleese's writing wasn't restricted merely to *Python*. He and Chapman had already written together for the ITV sitcom *Doctor in the House* in 1969, and Cleese contributed six solo scripts for one of its sequels, *Doctor at Large*, in 1971. One of the episodes, *No Ill Feeling!*, featured a prototype of the character of Basil Fawlty, a Mr Clifford who runs a suburban hotel, but more about Fawlty later.

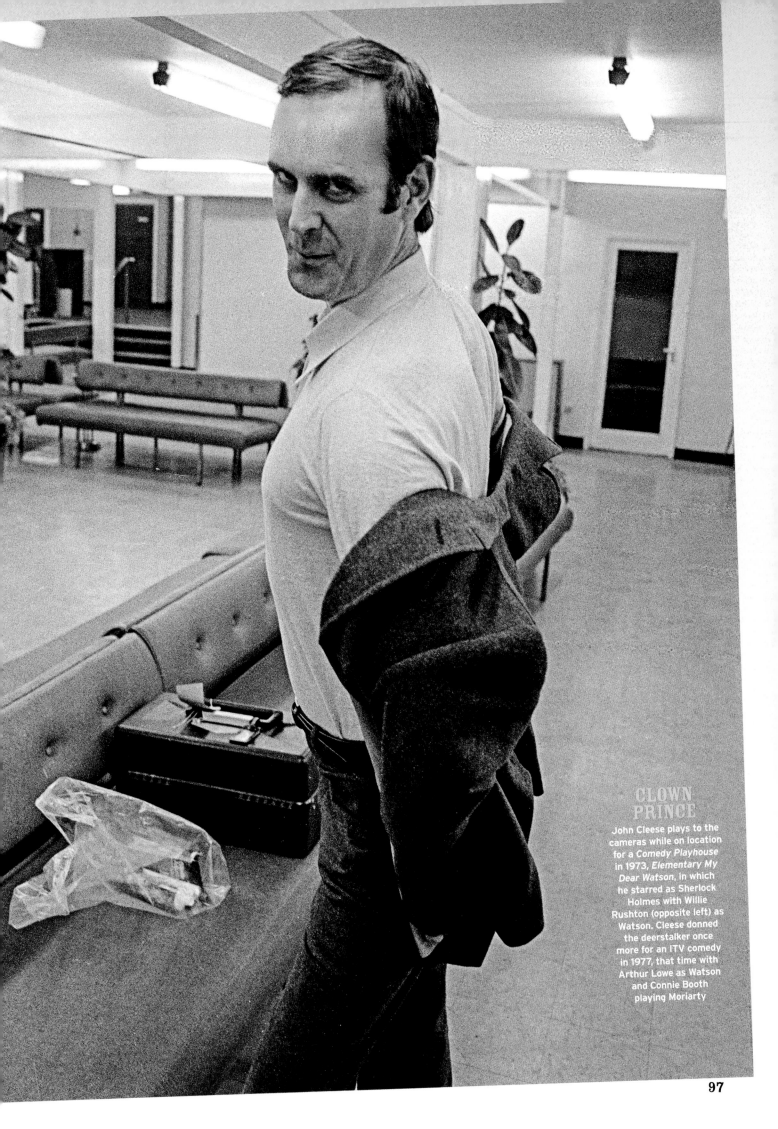

CLOWN PRINCE

John Cleese plays to the cameras while on location for a Comedy *Playhouse* in 1973, *Elementary My Dear Watson*, in which he starred as Sherlock Holmes with Willie Rushton (opposite left) as Watson. Cleese donned the deerstalker once more for an ITV comedy in 1977, that time with Arthur Lowe as Watson and Connie Booth playing Moriarty

6 *I dislike humour I can't believe in... It's got to be credible at the level it's offered* **9**

Cleese adapted and starred in a Chekhov story with Connie Booth (1974's *Romance with a Double Bass*), with whom he also wrote the first script for what was to become *Fawlty Towers*. So back to that Torquay hotel stay in 1970. As Cleese told *RT* in 1975, "The owner was the most wonderfully rude man I've ever met. He ticked off Terry Gilliam for his table manners, which he thought too American, and threw Eric Idle's briefcase out of the hotel, declaring that it probably contained a bomb."

He described Booth as "the best writing partner I could have – we always laugh at the same things", and explained that they tried to keep their situations somewhere within the bounds of possibility. "I dislike humour I can't believe in. No matter how daft something becomes it's got to be credible at the level it's offered and real to the characters involved in it."

Both Cleese and Booth believed that for comedy to succeed, it needed extraordinary time, care and effort. Cleese had been known to spend two days on half a dozen sentences, and then cut them all. He'd also tried to follow the Python tradition of packing in more than the usual quota of comic ideas: "I'm surprised how few there are in many half-hour series, and how much padding."

After that first six-part series in 1975, and the acclaim that built with every repeat, *Fawlty Towers* returned in 1979. It was honoured with an *RT* cover and an extensive interview by Guy Bellamy with the cast, as follows...

IT IS A DARK winter afternoon in Campden Hill Road, an untidy and depressing thoroughfare that links Kensington with Notting Hill Gate. But on the third floor of one of its many ugly buildings a happy reunion is taking place in a photographer's studio. Famous faces come in from the cold to find old friends waiting to greet them. It is a significant moment: several millions have waited three years for these people to get together again.

Fawlty Towers – to many people the funniest programme ever shown on television – is about to return with six new episodes, and John Cleese and Connie Booth arrive with five of the scripts that they have written. The sixth one has yet to be done.

Andrew Sachs, who plays the much-abused waiter Manuel, begins to read eagerly. The very first script gets off to a series of memorable laughs as a woman complains to Basil Fawlty that her half-eaten prawn cocktail is inedible. "Well, only half of it is inedible, apparently," says Basil, who agrees to knock half the price off the bill with further deductions tomorrow if she brings the other half up in the night.

"It's lovely to be doing it again," says Andrew, who is 48. "They're a lovely team. People always wonder what it's like working with John Cleese. They want to know if he is as mad as he seems."

John laughs: "Do you remember the time I almost brained you with a frying pan? I was trying a glancing blow but I got too close."

"The frying pan was dented afterwards," Andrew recalls proudly. "You also almost knocked my teeth out with a spoon."

"Be grateful that it's not a long run on stage," says John. "We only have to do it once. What are you worried about?"

It comes as a great surprise to discover that only six episodes of *Fawlty Towers* have ever been made. They have been shown three times in Britain and countless times all over the world. One channel on American television showed the whole lot in one evening.

ENGLAND   17-23 February 1979   Price 13p

RadioTimes

Fawlty service

Basil and Sybil Fawlty
(John Cleese and Prunella Scales)
assisted by Manuel and Polly
(Andrew Sachs and
Connie Booth) are back with
a new series of
'Fawlty Towers', BBC2.
Back feature: staff meeting

Although Radio Times has been fortunate to talk to the other surviving Pythons in 2019, Terry Jones was diagnosed with primary progressive aphasia in 2015. But his friend Michael Palin has kept in regular contact with him. "It's very important to keep Terry in the picture," he says. "He's still around, he's not disappeared, quite apart from the wonderful work he's done. I still go and see him, and there's still a bit of Terry there, the sparkle in the eye. He can't communicate, that's the problem, which is so ironic for someone who loved words and debate and jokes and opinions and ideas. A dementia like that doesn't suddenly stop or get better. But there's enough of Terry there to make me feel very grateful I can still go and see him."

And so we celebrate Jones's post-*Circus* career by drawing on a number of interviews he gave *Radio Times* over the years...

Consolidating his writing partnership with Michael Palin after *Flying Circus*, Terry Jones co-wrote the *Boys' Own*-flavoured comedy series *Ripping Yarns*, which was a critical and public hit for the duo between 1976 and 1979. But Jones had long been curious about directing, and when Python first went to the movies with *The Holy Grail* in 1975, he was able to realise his ambition. "Nobody else was particularly interested in directing," as he once put it, though he then got "cold feet" and "pulled Terry into it".

Jones went on to helm the follow-up films *Life of Brian* in 1979 and *The Meaning of Life* in 1983, minus Gilliam. Away from Python, he directed the Cynthia Payne-inspired comedy *Personal Services* (1987) and *Erik the Viking* (1989). He also penned a first draft of the screenplay for Jim Henson's fantasy

AUTHOR AND

DIRECTOR

HISTORY MAN

TERRY JONES

MYTH WORLD

Former Python Terry Jones makes his 'Jackanory' debut, reading and acting out his own tales of ogres, beasts and castles

Terry Jones published his first volume of children's stories shortly before his final Monty Python duties in the 1983 film *Monty Python's The Meaning of Life*. His latest collection, *Fantastic Stories*, was published in 1991, and now he will read and enact three of the tales for *Jackanory*, starting this week with *The Slow Ogre*.

"They're all set very much in the world of the traditional fairy story, with ogres and castles and talking beasts," says Jones. "Whenever I write a new story I try it out on my neighbours' son, Tom, to see if it works. My own kids are both grown up now, so they're not much use, but I find Tom a very reliable critic."

Although *Jackanory* has been running since 1965, this is Jones's first acquaintance with it. "I was at university when it started, and my children never watched much TV. But I think I've got a reasonable grasp of what makes for a good kids' story. You need a very strong storyline and you need to keep a surprise up your sleeve for the end.

"I loved reading as a kid. I was a great fan of Rupert the Bear, to the exclusion of almost everything else. Then, at 14, I went straight on to Ray Bradbury, which probably explains a lot."

RUPERT SMITH

The Slow Ogre Monday BBC1

---

film *Labyrinth* (1986).

His writing extended into literature, with books on history (*Chaucer's Knight, Medieval Lives, Barbarians*) jostling with children's stories such as *Fairy Tales, The Beast with a Thousand Teeth* and *Fantastic Stories*. The last book was adapted for *Jackanory* in 1993, when Jones told *Radio Times* that the stories were all set "in the world of the traditional fairy story, with ogres and castles and talking beasts.

"Whenever I write a new story I try it out on my neighbours' son, Tom, to see if it works. My own kids are both grown up now, but I find Tom a reliable critic."

Although *Jackanory* had been running since 1965, this was Jones's first acquaintance with the programme. "I was at university when it started, and my children never watched much TV. But I think I've got a reasonable grasp of what makes for a good kids' story. You need a very strong storyline and you need to keep a surprise up your sleeve for the end.

"I loved reading as a kid. I was a great fan of Rupert the Bear, to the exclusion of almost everything else. Then, at 14, I went straight on to Ray Bradbury, which probably explains a lot."

Moving slowly away from comedy (but not entirely; Jones could never resist a humorous treatment), he began to present history documentaries, with programmes about the Crusades, ancient inventions and Barbarians.

Previewing his 2000 BBC2 documentary *Gladiators: the Brutal Truth*, he pointed out that truth was stranger than fiction. "The history of gladiators has been blatantly lifted from the scripts of Monty Python. For example, in *Life of Brian* we staged a gladiatorial contest in which a feeble retiarius (or 'net-man') is faced by a formidable gladiator. We thought it would be fun if the net-man simply took to his heels and ran round and round the amphitheatre until the gladiator, weighed down by his armour, ended up having a heart attack. Bit of Theatre of the Absurd, or so we thought...

"However, while filming *Gladiators: the Brutal Truth*, we discovered that almost nothing we could dream up was too far from the truth. For example, occasionally Christians were thrown to the lions only to find that the poor animals were in such a pathetic state of health they didn't have the strength to finish anyone off. They might give the humans a terrible mauling, but they wouldn't kill them. Christians intent on martyrdom would grab the lions by their manes and stick their heads in their mouths in order to force the creatures to do their duty.

"And that would be just the day's warm-up. No, really! Throwing convicts to unpleasant deaths was strictly downmarket entertainment – restricted to the warm-up sessions. In *Life of Brian* we called it 'the Children's Matinee'. We thought we were joking...

"The gladiatorial contests of ancient Rome were very expensive operations. It was showbiz on a grand scale. And the executive producers were usually emperors."

To celebrate the Pythons' 40th anniversary in 2009, *Radio Times* interviewer Andrew Duncan visited Jones at his house near London's Hampstead Heath, where he and his Swedish partner Anna Soderstrom were living, with their days-old daughter Siri and their Yorkshire terrier Nancy. Here's an edited version of that article, which appeared in the 3 October 2009 edition of *RT*...

ON THE DOOR of his garage he's taped a colour picture of himself with a shovel and the words: "Every time your dog s***s on our driveway, we have to clear it up." In the sitting room there's an oil painting of him naked, playing the organ, done by an art student, which Jones bought, possibly against his better judgement. He rolls his eyes.

Jones, 67, looks youthful and fit. Relaxed and urbane, he laughs a lot, is convivially discursive, with a nonchalant and slightly contradictory air – most things, he claims, have happened to him by accident, yet he admits to being a control freak.

He met Anna, 41 years younger than him, five years ago at a book signing in Oxford where she was studying languages. He has a daughter Sally, 35, and son Bill,

---

FATHERLY TYPE

Posing for the *RT* cameras in his study at home in Hampstead, north-west London, in 2009, shortly after Jones, then 67, and his partner Anna had become parents to a baby girl, Siri. "Having a child who'll be loved, to parents who love each other, is the important thing," said Jones. Among the books on his shelf were volumes of his childhood favourite, *Rupert the Bear*

GLAD RAGS

Jones donned combat clobber to publicise *Gladiators: the Brutal Truth* in 2000

Death match

32, from his marriage to biochemist Alison Telfer.

We go to his study where he sits at a fading orange desk bought years ago for £1 on a Peckham street. He's just finished a libretto commissioned by the Royal Opera House, had his musical fantasy *Evil Machines* performed last year, has written children's books, poetry, an academic treatise on Chaucer, and on his computer is an article on Hampstead Heath.

The five remaining Pythons will receive a special Bafta on 15 October at a reunion event in New York, and there'll be a 105-minute theatrical presentation (as well as six one-hour specials on US TV) made by son Bill's company. "The BBC want to cut it down to an hour, which I worry will make it the same as any other documentary. They think audience attention span is so small they can only manage an hour."

The first *Monty Python's Flying Circus* show was inauspicious. The audience was mostly pensioners who thought they were coming to a real circus. "John Cleese muttered, 'This might be the first TV comedy with no laughs whatsoever.' It was the same with the films – the first showing of *The Holy Grail* was a disaster. Nobody laughed. One of the most awful evenings I've ever spent.

6 The Pythons work for a new generation: school kids are fans 9

Terry Jones 1942-
Lived here
Oedd yn byw yma

I suspect *Life of Brian* is overrated, although I think it's pretty good. It's easier to understand comedy if you're confident of people delivering it. You look at Morecambe and Wise now because you love Eric and Ernie, but it wasn't that funny, whereas the Pythons work for a new generation: school kids are fans."

He agrees with Michael Palin they wouldn't be commissioned today. "The BBC would want to see a test version and study demographics. They never liked or understood it. It was touch and go if they'd commission a second series."

The Pythons themselves got on well, he says. "We respected each other's writing, although John tried to get my goat. He's even more of a control freak than me, an odd person, which is why he's so wonderful. He doesn't really have a sense of humour, especially about himself, but he has a great gift for comedy. I felt the Pythons had to be the funniest thing on TV, and would make or break us.

"I'm not sure we influenced comedy. I think *Blackadder*, which was terrific, was a reaction against us.

"Humour can't change anything, but it can make people realise they're not alone." Likewise political protest. For years he's campaigned against the Iraq war. "It helps people if they think someone is at least talking about the criminal idiocy of it. I get my information from truthout. org. I can't bear TV news – the language follows the agenda of political elites. They talk about 'insurgents' and 'Islamic terrorists'. In the Second World War the same people were 'freedom fighters'."

Satire is not *always* effective. "Politicians love it: it makes them more famous. And series like *Till Death Us Do Part*, which [writer] Johnny Speight said was attacking prejudice, can increase it, I'm afraid. It gives a vocabulary to intolerance – 'Silly old moo'."

Unlike Cleese and Palin, Jones disappeared from public view, preferring to direct and write. "I'm writing a script at the moment." He pauses. "Actually, I'm doing three – the trouble is you spend so long on them and few get going. Also I find it hard to write movies. I've always been dissatisfied with them, and through the 90s I became distracted making historical documentaries for television. They're fascinating, but don't pay the bills.

"I'm proud and relieved the Pythons have lasted so long. It enabled me to do a lot of academic stuff because I didn't need to earn money."

HOLY GRAIL TO QUIXOTE, VIA BRAZIL

TERRY GILLIAM

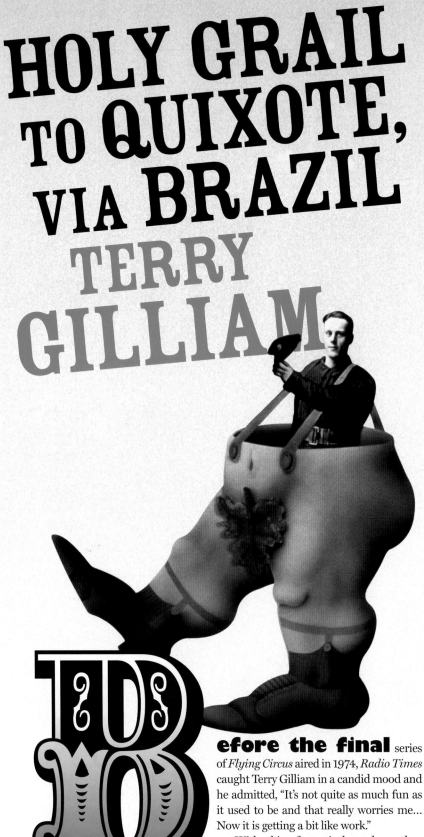

Before the final series of *Flying Circus* aired in 1974, *Radio Times* caught Terry Gilliam in a candid mood and he admitted, "It's not quite as much fun as it used to be and that really worries me... Now it is getting a bit like work."

With his fantastical and restless imagination, Gilliam was looking for new challenges, and they came quickly – with Gilliam co-directing the team's first proper film, *Monty Python and the Holy Grail* (1975), with Terry Jones. "Terry and I were great medievalists and couldn't wait to get in there," Gilliam once remarked.

Looking back today, Gilliam elaborates: "Terry and I ultimately divided up *Holy Grail*: he would spend more time with the others and I would make sure everything looked great." And despite fraught relations and plenty of learning on the job, *Grail* was shot in lightning time: "We did it in no time, 28 days or something ridiculous. We didn't know better; that was the advantage.

"When I look back at that film, the fact that we pulled it off in the time we did, considering we were up a mountain, in difficult situations, is really quite amazing. And I just think the others weren't used to trying to get things into a cinematic level of production value and all the things that make it. They were just used to doing sketches in bad lighting!"

The experience clearly didn't deter him. "No, that's why I did *Jabberwocky*. I didn't need them." Which explains why Gilliam didn't direct the Pythons in *Life of Brian*. "I thought, 'I don't want to direct these guys, they're a pain in the ass!'"

Gilliam's bid to get away from Python initially backfired with *Jabberwocky* in 1977. "Well, that's how stupid I can be," he laughs. "I make my first solo effort: it's a medieval film, a comedy, Michael Palin and Terry Jones are both in it, so three Pythons involved... and I'm not going to be compared to *Holy Grail*?! But it was trying to escape from just having to be funny all the time. I just wanted to do other things as well."

Letting go of Python must have proved trickier than he expected: Gilliam co-wrote his next venture, the time-travelling fantasy *Time Bandits* (1981), with Palin, who also guest-starred. Palin also featured in Gilliam's magnum opus, the critically acclaimed dystopian satire *Brazil* (1985). The film's anti-bureaucratic stance was mirrored in real life by Gilliam's battle with the studios over the film's length and downbeat ending.

Problems continued with his next film, the over-budget fantasy *The Adventures of Baron Munchausen* in 1988, which this time featured Eric Idle in a small role.

Paring back the budget for his next two releases, Gilliam drew praise from critics for the modern-day Grail adventure *The Fisher King* (1991) and the sci-fi drama *Twelve Monkeys* (1995). Then came the psychedelic *Fear and Loathing in Las Vegas* (1998) and the fairy-tale-inspired *The Brothers Grimm* (2005).

Profiling him in 2003, *RT* film critic Barry Norman wrote: "Gilliam is a one-off, a romantic who doesn't see things like anyone else. He will not, he says, accept life's limitations and that immediately brings him into conflict with mainstream

> **We did Grail in no time, 28 days or something ridiculous. We didn't know better**

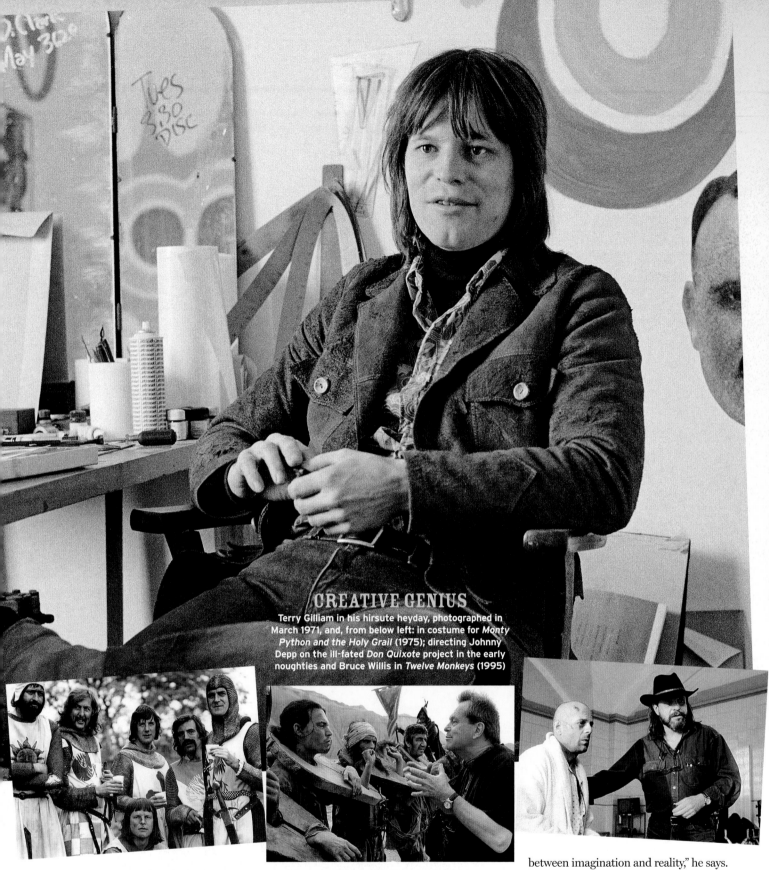

cinema, especially Hollywood, which wants us to accept its own idea of life's limitations."

At that time, Gilliam's long-term project, *The Man Who Killed Don Quixote*, had foundered – and become the subject of a fascinating film entitled *Lost in La Mancha*. It documents insurmountable obstacles including an injured star, the location turning out to be on the flight path of Nato jets, and a flash flood that washed away the set and damaged equipment.

Norman continued: "You felt it could only have happened to Gilliam. But by the same token only Gilliam could have got up, dusted himself off and vowed to buy his screenplay back from the producers so that he could try again. If that seems like tilting at windmills, well, it's what Gilliam does. Like Cervantes's novel, a Gilliam movie usually involves some bizarre quest, a touch of metaphor, comments on the state of the world and struggling through. So he identifies strongly with Quixote, especially his 'relentless determination to do the impossible'."

But what does Gilliam think links his movies? "They're all about the battle between imagination and reality," he says. "My films aren't fantasy because there's always reality that's pulling you back. For most people I think that's what your life is. Between your dreams, your ambitions, and the reality: you need both of them. And I think that's what I do. The tension is what is interesting."

The Man Who Killed Don Quixote finally saw the light of day in 2018, receiving a standing ovation at Cannes. As we went to press, it was still awaiting a general release date due to legal reasons.

A **n integral** member of the team for 20 years, Graham Chapman died from cancer on the eve of Monty Python's 20th anniversary, aged 48. At his memorial service in the Great Hall at St Bartholomew's Hospital, John Cleese broke the sombre mood with a shocking joke, adding, "Gray would have wanted it this way. Really. Anything for him but mindless good taste. And that's what I'll always remember about him – apart, of course, from his Olympian extravagance. He was the prince of bad taste. He loved to shock. In fact, Gray, more than anyone I knew, embodied and symbolised all that was most offensive and juvenile in Monty Python. And his delight in shocking people led him on to greater and greater feats. I like to think of him as the pioneering beacon that beat the path along which fainter spirits could follow."

Eric Idle "If you think of Python as a family, Graham was much more like a mother. So they would say, 'What does John want to do?' And he'd say, 'Well, I'll ask John.' And they'd say, 'You come back and tell us whether John's going to do any more or not.' So he could be in the middle like that. He could tell people what was really going on, or what people wanted, and make things happen. He was also a lovely actor, a really fine actor in the films. He was quite a loony performing for television, as I remember. He enjoyed playing loonies."

Terry Jones "I remember him going round a bar in Glencoe kissing everybody, when we were doing *Monty Python and the Holy Grail*. He eventually got thrown out." *See the obituary Jones wrote for RT in 1989, opposite*

Terry Gilliam "I just remember Graham being from another planet. It was nice to work with an alien! His view of the world and how he behaved was exciting because it was dangerous. He'd be in a restaurant and suddenly, for whatever reason, take a dislike... 'That couple over there at that table...' The next moment, he's crawled over and is under their table licking their feet. Now that is not a healthy way to survive and he used to get beaten up a lot. He just came from another place and it was nice to have someone who was so purely eccentric. That's the word I'm missing in modern Britain: 'eccentricity'. Where are the eccentrics now? Graham was one of the last of the true eccentrics."

Michael Palin "A great example of Graham's approach was when we were filming *Holy Grail* in Scotland. Graham drank a lot and he was always the last to leave the bar. He also had a bit of a thing about [the actress] Betty Marsden, who'd been on various shows and all that. You're trying to get to sleep at night and Graham comes up from the bar and starts shouting, 'Betty Marsden?' in the corridor. 'Betty Marsden? I'm going to bed now. I'm available.' This happened about three or four nights and after the fourth night I said, 'Graham, the Betty Marsden thing, honestly... we're trying to get some sleep. We're busy tomorrow. Can you not...' 'Ooh,' he says, 'I'm terribly sorry,' because he was very polite. And that was the end of it, until the next morning when I found a piece of paper under my door. I picked it up and I opened it, and there, written on it, was: 'Betty Marsden.'"

REMEMBERING
GRAHAM
CHAPMAN
1941-1989

SHADES OF GRAY

Chapman, with pipe in hand, at a 1974 Python meeting. "Graham had a sort of quiet, abstracted but brilliant, sharp silliness that no one else could quite come up with," says Palin

Carol Cleveland "It was very sad when we lost Graham. He was a lovely man. It took me a while to get used to his overt drinking and homosexuality, which I felt slightly uncomfortable with in the beginning. But by the time we'd completed the second series, I'd got to know him better and discovered what a kind, caring and generous man he was."

John Cleese "I remember Graham going up to receive an award on behalf of the group, which was being presented mysteriously by Reginald Maudling [former Conservative Chancellor of the Exchequer]. When Graham got to the foot of the stairs leading up to the stage he fell to the ground and crawled towards him, screaming. Maudling took four steps back and just handed him the award."

VOICE OVER

Graham Chapman died of cancer earlier this month. A fellow Python remembers him

TERRY JONES

‘When first I came across Graham it was as a footnote in a programme for the Cambridge Footlights revue: *Cambridge Circus* in 1963. Graham wasn't actually in the show, because he was off completing his medical training. There was, however, a drawing of him, and it stuck in my mind because I remember thinking that the avuncular, pipe-smoking man in the portrait didn't look like someone who could make me laugh.

The next time I came across him, I thought exactly the same thing. He was performing in *At Last the 1948 Show* with John Cleese, Marty Feldman and Tim Brooke-Taylor. My eyes kept going to Graham as I thought 'he still doesn't look like someone who could make me laugh' and yet he was. I could understand why John made me laugh, and I could see why Marty and Tim made me laugh, but I just couldn't see where Graham was coming from at all.

He was the most off-the-wall of the Pythons. The most unpredictable and the most unfathomable.

During the Python days, his mind would produce leaps of hilarious illogic that came out of nowhere and surprised us into laughter. It was he who came up with my personal favourite suggestions for a title for the TV shows: *Owl-Stretching Time* and *The Toad-Elevating Moment*. And I can never forget his performance as one of two ladies in the launderette discussing the problems of flushing unwanted budgies down the loo. ('They breed in the sewers and you get huge flocks of soiled budgies flying out of the loo infringing people's personal freedom.')

Yet there was always the sober, perfectly rational side to Graham. When we were filming *The Life of Brian* in Tunisia Graham's main piece of luggage was a huge suitcase packed with medical supplies. Every day, after a gruelling time playing the lead in the film, Graham would retire to his hotel room and hold an open surgery for anyone who needed it – not just cast and crew but Tunisian extras, people he met in the street and hotel staff as well.

Douglas Adams recently said that Graham was extremely . . . in fact he was one of the most extremely people he knew. And I think he's right. Graham didn't do anything by halves. If he was setting up as the unit doctor, he became the unit doctor and practised it without thought of personal inconvenience. When he drank he drank until he recognised that he was an alcoholic. When he decided to stop drinking, he stopped drinking, and not only that but told everybody his story. When he decided that he preferred men to ladies, he espoused his sexual inclination as cause as much as preference, and made sure everybody understood and knew that this was how he felt.

Graham was a surprising man. In the same way that he surprised us into laughter, he surprised us into love for him.’

BBC1 will be celebrating 20 years of Monty Python next month

21-27 OCTOBER 1989

ANNIVERSARIES

10TH

To accompany a *documentary that caught up with the Pythons in 1979, while they were filming Life of Brian in Tunisia, a Radio Times feature took us back to the show's early days...* Stepping out unrhythmically in the water towards the sandy shores of Shell Bay, south Dorset, is a wasted, bearded, exhausted old man in a tattered suit and tie. He lurches forward, a ragged, wretched wreck of a human being, victim of some dreadful disaster with an achingly urgent message... ready, it seems, to take his last breath and with it to pronounce on the nature of the horror pressing close. "It's..."

It's is the first title of a possible series yet to be conceived, written and performed by six men eating lunch in the Light of Kashmir restaurant in Hampstead. It is early May, 1969, and they are reaching agreement on the kind of comedy they are not going to conceive, write and perform. They will have no front man, no dancing girls; no resident musicians, no stars and no respect for traditional comedy conventions. For their second title, they choose *It's Not*.

The first script for a new comedy series, now called *Owl Stretching Time*, arrives at the BBC on Thursday 19 June. Throughout this script, ideas are delivered from sketch to sketch like postcards. Sometimes the messages are read out by announcers, as in "And now for something completely different... a man with three buttocks".

Three scripts later, it is late August. Waiting in Studio 6 at Television Centre are 150 props including one body of a sheep, two revolvers, four white mice and two long thin French loaves. A camera crew under John Howard Davies has 90 minutes to record the 30-minute videotape into which five minutes of the edited location filming and over two and a half minutes of Terry Gilliam's animation will be slotted. It is time for Palin, Jones, Idle, Cleese and Chapman to adopt the personalities of 40 different characters, their costumes, their make-up, their voices, on film and videotape in front of a live audience of 400 for the first time, in a new BBC1 comedy series called *Monty Python's Flying Circus...*

John Cleese: "The beginning, with the old man coming towards the camera, wasn't symbolic – we just liked the idea of wasting the audience's time. I mean, provided you do it in a way that makes them laugh. The whole thing to involve someone in a very lengthy walk or movement towards camera and culminate it in them simply saying 'It's...' It was also our irritation that at that time, everyone who ever got a comedy show called it 'It's John Cleese' or 'It's Michael Palin.'"

Michael Palin: "It's always very difficult to start or end a show. I mean, *Python* was hopelessly adrift on beginnings and endings... And the more we could sort of confuse people, the easier it would be to get away with the fact that we didn't have any beginnings or endings.

"Documentaries will always begin 'Tonight we're looking at'. Or a man standing in front of a building with a microphone. The 'It's Man' fitted into that extremely well because it was obvious that he had fled some terror and the terror was never explained. You just saw the end of an event – a man in deep trouble. And happily it did turn neatly into an ending in that he would implore the audience for help. 'Let me into your homes, please.'"

> **The It's Man would implore, "Let me into your homes"**
> MICHAEL PALIN

In 20 years *Monty Python had gone from obscure late-night show to national treasure, so what did the reunited team think? Shortly before Graham Chapman's death in 1989, they told RT...*

So how does it feel to be an institution? Terry Gilliam is inconsolable. "It's the last nail in the coffin. It's being proclaimed an old fart at last." Doleful Pythons concur noddingly. Eric Idle says: "One minute you're banned; the next minute you're on top of some sort of pillar. We've gone from cult to institution in 20 years." "Destitution is what I call it," is Graham Chapman's reaction.

Terry Jones sighs. "We're a museum piece." This is true – the Pythons are now an exhibit in the Museum of Broadcasting in New York.

Cleese is still simmering over a recent newspaper article that concentrated, disproportionately, in his view, on the internecine rivalry in the old days. "Mind you," says Michael Palin, "Terry did throw a typewriter at John once. We got it out of his skull quite quickly, though." Doctor Chapman, who was in charge of the operation, adds, "After some moderate surgery, yes." Jones is indignant. "I never threw a typewriter at him! It was a chair." Cleese can't remember the incident.

One-time train spotter and Python diarist Palin has instant recall of another moment. "We were doing the Long John Silver Football Team. No studio cars, of course: there wasn't the budget. So in my Mini I had John and Graham, two of the largest comedy writers in the country, squeezed into the back, Terry Jones on my left, all of us with parrots and wooden legs. And I had to go to the bank – it's always the wrong time when you're filming – so I went into the one at Shepherd's Bush. And they all decided to come in with me. So there was this silly parade of Long John Silvers at the cash till, and I said to the cashier, 'Can I cash a cheque?' She just looked up, totally unfazed, and said, 'Yes, if you've got a cheque card.'"

Terry Jones has taken off his trousers on more high streets and Yorkshire moors than any other person in Britain. He recalls the Being a Mason sketch. "I think it was the six of us dressed like bankers, walking

LONDON (BBC Radio London: page 70) 16-22 June 1979 Price 14p

RadioTimes

It's...

...the Old Man of the Sea?
The Creature from the Black Lagoon perhaps?
No, it's Michael Palin, ten years after stumbling on to our screens in the very first 'Monty Python's Flying Circus'. In a rare reunion 'The Pythons', Chapman, Cleese, Gilliam, Idle, Jones and Palin look back, forwards and sideways at themselves, Wednesday BBC1.
Back feature: they think, therefore they are

up the little hill that leads to St Paul's Cathedral. For some reason we decided to film this with a camera in a passing car, so there was no sign that we were filming. So these six respectable bankers or City gents suddenly dropped their trousers and started hopping up the street. And nobody took a blind bit of notice... they probably thought we *were* Masons."

John Cleese smiles suddenly. "My happiest memory of Python is reading out the cheese sketch to the others." Graham Chapman starts to laugh at another memory. "For pure joy, my very favourite is the Undertaker sketch, with John coming in with his mother's dead body in a sack. John and I laughed more while we were writing that than anything we ever did, I think. We had to tell our mothers that the other one had written it. The BBC got a bit jumpy after that one."

"Python," sums up Michael Palin, "for some reason or other is lodged in the national subconscious, and will be there for a long while, I suppose."

Graham Chapman, who had cancer, died a few days after this chat with RT. Interviewer Tony Bilbow wrote: "Although he was obviously tired he was generous with his time and his contribution to this piece, and he laughed a lot. He was much loved and will be greatly missed."

30TH

As Flying Circus *marked 30 years in 1999, John Cleese talked about reuniting for a Python evening...*

Settling on a large white sofa at his west London home, John Cleese explains that a mellowness has overtaken Pythons everywhere as the bus pass looms. "We get on much better. It is different now." He frequently sees Michael Palin, but has seen the others hardly at all, though recently four of them went out to dinner. "We realised that we laugh more when we are together than we do with anyone else." In the old days, they used to argue like cats and dogs about their sketches. "As you get older it doesn't matter quite so much. When you have been writing for 35 years it is so much easier to make concessions. You realise that this stuff you cared about so tremendously didn't work very well and perhaps the others were right."

Indeed, when he looks at old Python programmes now he finds them soberingly patchy. "I usually think three things are truly hilarious and a certain amount which must have been original at the time is OK... But we were doing things in a new way. No one can remember now the sense of liberation when the rules were broken for the first time."

In fact, they had their first reunion last March, at a comedy festival in Aspen, Colorado, where they sat on stage for a question-and-answer session. "Eddie Izzard came on with us and answered the early questions. People thought: 'Which one was he?'" They also brought on stage an urn supposedly containing the ashes of Graham Chapman, the deceased Python. Only when it was accidentally knocked over and the ashes went flying did the quietly horrified audience realise this was a characteristic jape.

The reunion was so enjoyable that they even decided to do a stage tour. "Afterwards we had a typical Python meeting. We all agreed on the tour, then people left the room and changed their minds in eight hours... So the whole thing petered out."

'We laugh more when we are together than we do with anyone else'
JOHN CLEESE

When the BBC suggested an anniversary evening there was a happier response and all bar Eric were able to make a space in their diaries. The other four have been meeting to write a script for new material to link the evening, which features a documentary on the Python phenomenon hosted by Eddie Izzard, a programme on the Python songs and a spoof Palin travelogue around west London. "Michael and Terry Jones did a rough draft, then I did two more drafts and we had a meeting. Then Michael did a little more writing. I tried to give structure with the links." Whatever the working method, the result is, he says, very Pythonic.

"We would have been much stronger if Graham Chapman was still with us, but he was a lazy b****r. He didn't get in and row with us. He would sit on the bank and occasionally shout wacky things, which would give us a new sense of direction. But Graham was a really marvellous actor and if he had not had alcoholism problems we would be much more aware of him."

Cleese is writing scripts for three film comedies, but he adds, "The trouble with writing comedy is that you don't learn anything from it other than how to write comedy. I'm only happy now if I'm learning something." For this reason, he plans to learn German. "I have wanted to learn German for 45 years. It appeals to me. German writers are so much more interesting than any of the others..."

FAMILY REUNION
Celebrating the Pythons' 20th anniversary in 1989. Chapman spoke to *Radio Times* a matter of days before he died of cancer on 4 October

50TH

The two covers that Terry Gilliam has created for *Radio Times* are separated by 45 years, and a lot has changed in the design world in that time. His cover for 1974 (above) was based on his animations for *Flying Circus*. "Yeah, those were just literally all cut out. I would go into books, I'd find images that I liked and then take them down to a place just off Regent Street called Atlas Photography – they don't exist there any more. And I marked it up and they'd blow it up to the sizes I would need for the animation and then I'd cut out, colour in and go to work." He fashioned our brand-new front page (overleaf), celebrating 50 years of Monty Python, using Photoshop. "I just dig around. I get images and stick them together. It's much easier than cutting out. And it's easier to manipulate. When I make a mistake, I can fix it easily."

40TH

In 2009 the 40th anniversary was marked by an interview with Terry Jones (see p104), with him choosing his top five sketches. They were the Life of Tchaikovsky featuring an escapologist pianist ("I was so pleased with myself hitting the piano keys at the right time"), the Lumberjack Song, the Spanish Inquisition ("When Mike first read it out to me, I couldn't see how he'd thought of it"), the Batley Townswomen's Battle of Pearl Harbor and Spam ("Because I didn't have to learn it. I just read it off a blackboard").

So Terry, looking back on your life and career, what were the defining influences on the young Gilliam?
Living in the country [in Minnesota], radio and books were what it was all about because we didn't have television. I read a lot. There's a writer who nobody knows in this country: Albert Payson Terhune. He wrote stories about faithful dogs in the Highlands. And radio was fantastic… great sound effects, great stories. *The Fat Man*, you couldn't do that now! The Larger Than Normal Man… And *The Shadow*… "Only the Shadow knows! Hoo-ha!"

How did you become a strip cartoonist?
From early on I would draw cartoons, I just did it. Cartoons are great because they're quick, easy, and people laugh, and so you get immediate feedback. It's not like writing a novel where you spend years. I ended up editing a magazine

[*Help!*] with Harvey Kurtzman, who gave us *Mad* comics. *Mad* was a huge influence because it was the first time I really saw satire or pastiche. Harvey liked what I was doing and I ended up in New York working with him.

Your first contact with a future Python was with John Cleese. What were your first impressions of him?
Cambridge Circus had come to New York on the coat-tails of *Beyond the Fringe* and there was John, Graham Chapman, Bill Oddie, Tim Brooke-Taylor, David Hatch. He stood out: John has always stood out, there's no way around that. He was outrageous. He was so funny. I mean, John has never changed…

In England, you produced animations for *Do Not Adjust Your Set* before joining Python…
What's wonderful is it just

came together organically. And the BBC was far, far less interested in the rest of us, it was John's show as far as the BBC was concerned. We made it clear after a while it was six people doing this thing!

Would *Flying Circus* get made today?

We've always been rather diverse. Python was way ahead. We were all in drag, we were transitional before anybody else. We took the p*** out of just everything, and that was important.

Was it your agenda to turn comedy upside down?

No, I don't think we thought as grandly as that. We were much more pragmatic. Our big thing was to get rid of the punchline. That made a difference because then the

sketch was about what was going on within it, and it also, I suppose, created the space for me to connect the sketches. So things didn't ever end, they sort of went on into something else.

Did you always want to direct?

Somewhere along the line, yeah, it happened, way back when I don't know...

And which moment makes you laugh whenever you think about it?

The Fish Slapping Dance. It's very hard not to laugh. And I can't explain why. If you sit and try to analyse why it's funny, you can't. But it's pointless. It *is* funny!

7-13 SEPTEMBER 2019
RadioTimes

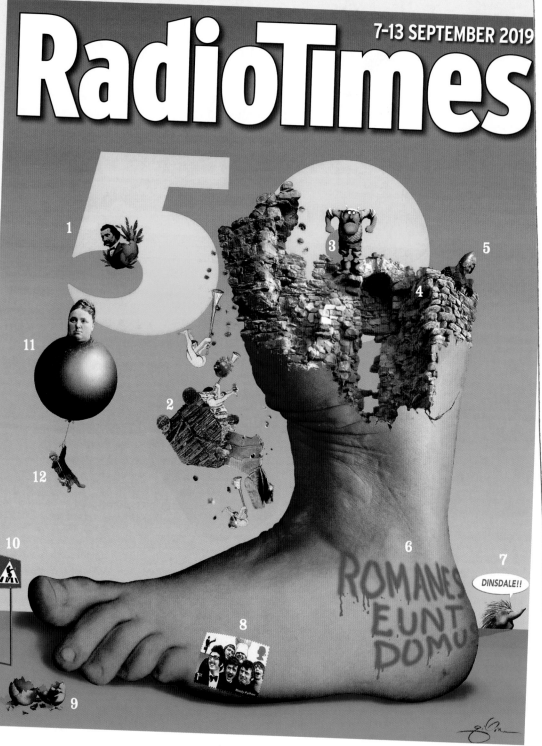

FOOT NOTES

1 CHICKEN MAN First appeared in the opening titles to series two of *Monty Python's Flying Circus*.

2 THE TROJAN RABBIT "This is from *Holy Grail*. And it's falling with all the trumpeters. It's about collapse and this is very much about decay."

3 GUMBY "This is really about the stupidity of the age we're living in, where Gumby is triumphant."

4 CASTLE "I own this in Italy, this bit of masonry. I own a bit of a castle and this is part of the keep that was there, which I just included to show the leg and foot crumbling."

5 TAUNTER "I had to get John Cleese in there somewhere as the Taunter from *Holy Grail*. But the Taunter is silent. Is this us? Is it because we're not allowed to taunt people now? That's like mocking them. And mocking is definitely out because it might cause offence to somebody somewhere on the planet."

6 GRAFFITI "I got the graffiti from *Life of Brian*." The slogan is the one Brian paints on the wall of the Governor's palace to prove himself worthy of being a member of the People's Front of Judea.

7 "**DINSDALE** is the threat somewhere in the distance." Spiny Norman was a giant hedgehog imagined by gangster Dinsdale Piranha in *Flying Circus*.

8 2015 STAMP "I thought, if we're going to have the old crumbling edifice of Python, let's get us when we were young. That's when we were first-class comedians rather than shabby old farts."

9 BROKEN EGG HEAD "More about the stupidity of the world!"

10 SIGN "This is now in cities in Europe, where they have signs for silly walking. That represents Python expanding into Europe."

11 BALLOON "Everything else is collapsing, the only thing that's rising is obesity [laughs]. The one thing we can guarantee in the modern world is that."

12 "... And yet dangling from it, rising, is a **CHILD**, the only one who will speak the truth any more. No political correctness with that kid, she says only what she sees..."